USBORNE
MONEY
FOR BEGINNERS

Written by
Eddie Reynolds, Matthew Oldham
and **Lara Bryan**

Illustrated by
Marco Bonatti

Contents

What is money?	4
How money moves	6
Money around the world	8
Money customs	10

Chapter 1: How money works   13
What makes bills, coins and anything else count
as money? And why do we all trust it?

Chapter 2: The story of money   23
Money has existed since long before the first coins
were made, and over the centuries it has taken
on many unusual forms. How did all this come about?

Chapter 3: In the bank   35
Almost every adult has a bank account – but why?
What do banks actually do? Are there any alternatives?
And was it really the banks' fault that the world
suffered a financial meltdown in 2008?

Chapter 4: Earning and borrowing   53
Don't have any money? No problem! Almost anyone
can get a hold of *some* money, by working for it,
or borrowing from someone who has it.

Chapter 5: Spending, growing and giving 71
Some people spend everything they have very quickly.
Others prefer to save up. If you have money to spare,
should you give it all away to charity?

Chapter 6: Governments and money 89
Taxes, deficits, inflation, deflation, quantitative easing
– what does it all mean, and who's in charge?

Chapter 7: Big questions 105
How to be a billionaire, whether money can buy
happiness, how to make the world a fairer place – and
other important questions that nobody knows the
answers to – *yet*.

What next? 121

Glossary 122
Index 125
Acknowledgements 128

Usborne Quicklinks

For links to websites where you can visit a virtual bank,
see money from around the world, watch video clips about how
money works and find games and activities to help you manage
your money, go to the Usborne Quicklinks website at

www.usborne.com/quicklinks

and type in the keywords 'money for beginners'.

Children, please ask a grown-up before going
online and follow the internet safety
guidelines at the Usborne Quicklinks website.
Children should be supervised online.

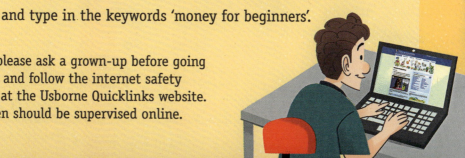

What is money?

Even people who deal with money as part of their job, such as bankers, accountants and economists, don't all agree what money actually *is*. The simplest (but slightly incomplete) answer is that it's anything that's accepted as payment.
In theory, this means all kinds of things.

Unfortunately, not many people will accept stickers or carrots as payment. Instead, there are two forms of money that most people use every day – **cash** and **electronic money**.

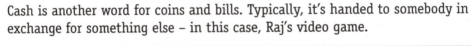

Unlike cash, electronic money (or e-money) isn't a physical thing – it's money stored electronically. Anyone with a **bank account** has e-money. Different devices can be used to access e-money to pay for things.

When you pay with e-money, no physical money changes hands. Instead, the e-money is sent from the bank account of the person paying to the account of the person (or business) selling.

Behind the scenes, the process of moving e-money from one account to another can be quite complicated.

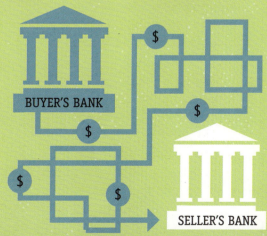

How money moves

Money flows between people constantly. When money moves from one person to another, it's known as an **exchange** or **transaction**. Here are the main ways it happens.

Earning
Most people **earn** money by doing a job that somebody **pays** them for. Find out more in chapter 4.

Spending
People **spend** money they earn on things they need, such as food and electricity, and stuff they want, such as books and treats. There's more on spending in chapter 5.

Taxation
People can't keep all the money they make. Everyone has to give some to the government to help pay for **public services**, such as schools and hospitals. This is known as **taxation**.

Find out more in chapter 6.

Wahoo! I've been paid. Think of all the things I could do with the money...

What if I need *more* money?

Maybe I could borrow it.

Donating

Give money to protect coral reefs against pollution!

Some organizations and charities rely on people **giving** them money. Giving money to a cause is known as **donating**. Find out more in chapter 5.

Investing

Investing is when someone spends money on something to make *more* money from it eventually.

I bought this piece of art. Hopefully it'll be worth more in the future, then I can sell it and make some money.

There are many different ways to invest. Find out more on pages 78-81.

Borrowing and lending

When people can't afford to do something, they can sometimes **borrow** money from somewhere else, such as a bank.

I borrowed money to buy a house.

This type of money is known as a **loan**. All loans have to be paid back. There's more about borrowing money in chapter 4.

All these transactions and exchanges take place between people, businesses, organizations, and even governments. *Most* money moves in this way, but not *all* of it...

Stealing

Another way money moves is when it's stolen, which is of course **illegal**. In the last year alone, hundreds of billions of dollars worth of money was stolen worldwide. There's more about money crimes on pages 66-67.

Mwahaha, I just hacked into 50 people's bank accounts – now their money is all **MINE**!

Ahem, I heard that!

Money around the world

Nobody knows *exactly* how much cash and e-money there is in the world. It exists in so many different currencies that it's hard to calculate. In 2017, the US government estimated that there's slightly over **80 trillion US dollars** out there. That amount changes every day.

If you had 80 trillion US dollars (US$), you could buy...

...around 350 million houses in Quebec, at 300,000 Canadian dollars (C$) each.

That's almost enough to give everybody in Canada 10 homes.

...160 billion flights from Paris to New York and back (US$490 each).

You'd be up in the air for longer than humans have even existed!

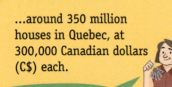

NORTH AMERICA

...1.3 trillion microwave ovens in Ohio (US$55 each).

If you stacked them, the pile would reach further than the Sun!

...160 trillion rolls of toilet paper in Bolivia (14 Bolivian dollars for a pack of four).

Enough to cover South America in over 20 layers of toilet paper.

SOUTH AMERICA

Canadian, US and Bolivian dollars are different **currencies**, even though they're all called *dollar*. There are lots of other currency names too, such as the euro (€), which is used in 19 countries in Europe.

There are currently 180 currencies in use across nearly 200 countries.

A single unit of one currency, such as 1 US dollar, is rarely worth the same as one unit of another currency, such as 1 Bolivian dollar.

In China the main currency is the yuan. In March 2021, 1 yuan was worth...

...around 11 ruble – the currency used in Russia.

...around 8 denar – the currency used in North Macedonia.

...around 6 birr – the currency used in Ethiopia.

...around 2 rand – the currency used in South Africa.

Turn to pages 20-21 to find out why exchange rates change all the time.

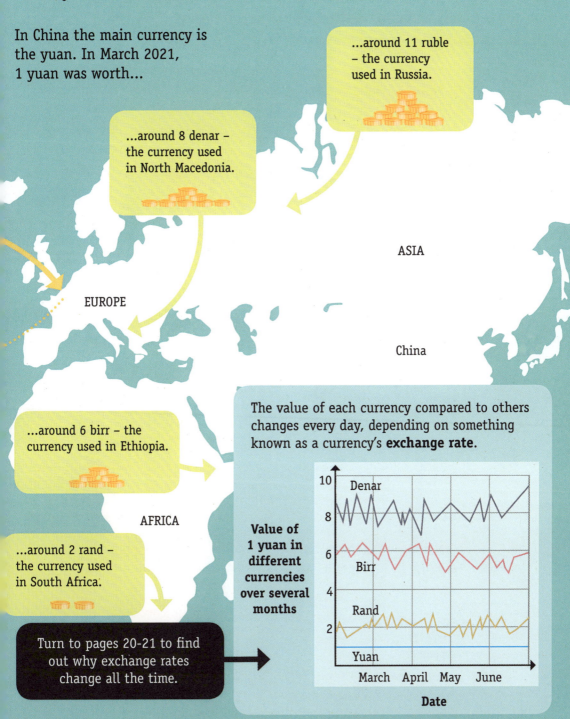

The value of each currency compared to others changes every day, depending on something known as a currency's **exchange rate**.

Value of 1 yuan in different currencies over several months

Throughout the rest of this book, prices and amounts of money are all shown in the same currency (US dollars), to make them easier to compare.

9

Money customs

People follow all sorts of rules when they handle and talk about money – often without realizing it. These change over time, and vary from country to country, and even family to family.

In some places, such as a supermarket, prices tend to be set...

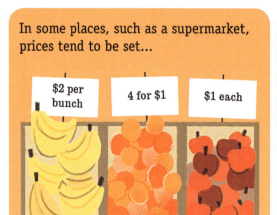

...and in others they aren't. Discussing a price is known as **negotiating**.

Sometimes, everyone pays their share...

...at other times, one person may pay for everything.

Giving a little extra money in exchange for someone's service, is known as a **tip**.

Americans expect big tips – 20% is typical – whereas in China people don't tip at all.

In Korea and Japan, people hand over money and gifts using two hands, as a sign of respect.

Talking about money

Lots (and lots!) of people worry about money, regardless of how much or little they feel they have. Sharing information with people you trust can be a good way of picking up useful advice.

But talking about money is sometimes seen as rude. This is because it's often a personal, even emotional topic.

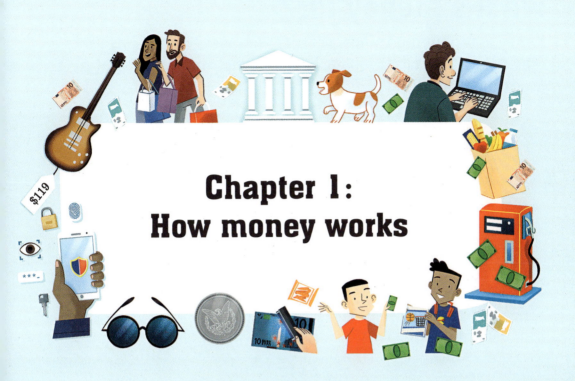

Chapter 1: How money works

Money is everywhere – whether you think of it as pieces of metal, sheets of paper, or as numbers in a bank account. And yet, most people use it every day without thinking about what it is or how it works.

You can't use just *anything* as money. It has to have some very specific features to make it valuable. Read on to find out more.

What's money for?

Money is for buying things, isn't it? Well, yes – but it has other uses, too. If it was just about buying something, you might not need money at all...

This way of buying something is called **bartering**, and you don't need money to do it. But how can you barter if only one person has what the other one wants?

This is where money comes in handy. People nearly always want money, so you can nearly always use it to buy what you want.

Experts say that when people use money to buy things and trade with each other, they're using it as a **medium of exchange**. But there are other ways to use money. You could also *save* it to use at a later date. Or *collect* it until you have more.

When money is used in this way, experts say it's being used as a **store of value**. It's only possible to *save* money because it keeps on being worth something.

People also use money to *measure value*, in the same way they use minutes and seconds to measure time. This makes it easier to work out what you can afford to buy, and to compare how much different things are worth.

Experts call this using money as a **unit of account**.

15

Easy money

Money would stop working if it was difficult to use. It's no coincidence that cash and e-money are used all over the world, but carrots, say, aren't. Money has certain attributes that make it excellent at what it does. The things that work best as money are...

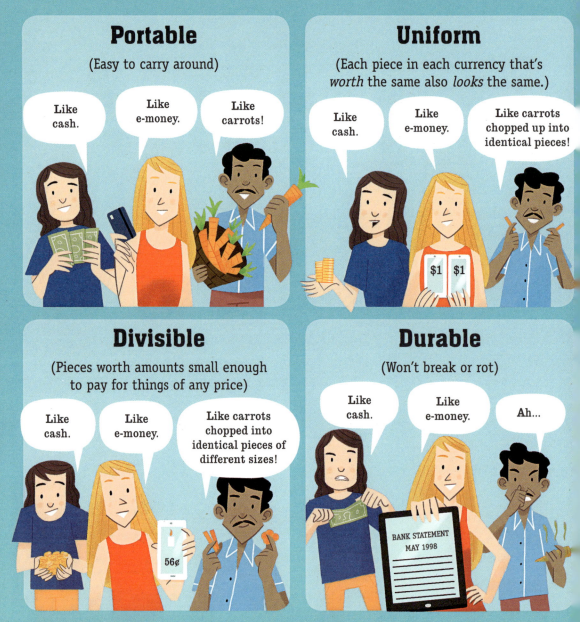

In practice, even cash and e-money aren't *perfect*. Bills can tear, coins can wear down, credit cards can snap, and computer failures at banks can make e-money disappear. But most of the time, all these work just fine.

Liquid money

Money flows easily from person to person and from business to business. Nearly everyone is happy to accept it as a form of payment, so it can be used to buy nearly anything. This quality is known as **liquidity**.

The value of money

Money isn't valuable in the same way as food, shelter and water – humans *can* live without it. Coins, bills and e-money only have value for a few specific reasons:

1. It's the law. Today's money is what's known as **fiat money**. This means it's only valuable because governments have set laws that *say* it's valuable.

To help people trust these laws, most governments share responsibility for the money in their countries with a separate organization known as a **central bank** – in the US, it's called the **Federal Reserve** (see chapter 6.)

2. The Federal Reserve and the Government limit the money supply.

Imagine a world in which photographs of cash could be used as cash...

This may *seem* fair, as everybody gets money. But if that happened, the original coin – and the photos of it – would *lose all value*.

If everyone could create unlimited amounts of money, people wouldn't *need* it from each other, so they wouldn't exchange it for things.

In the real world, where only a limited amount of money is available...

There's only one coin to share between three, so the coin is in demand, making it valuable.

3. Cash can only be made in specific places, under very secure conditions.

To make it hard for people to create their own unlimited supply of money, coins and bills are designed to be easy to identify, but difficult to copy exactly. Here are some typical design features.

Intricate patterns

Raised print on bills

Ridges and lettering around the edges (on some coins)

Hidden designs that can only be detected using UV light

However clever the designs, criminals can still produce fake, or **counterfeit**, bills and coins. But it's very difficult. If a bill has all the features of a genuine bill, it's almost certainly been made legally. So you can *trust* it.

Digital value

Although e-money doesn't have a physical form, we still trust it has value for the same three reasons.

1) E-money can be exchanged for cash, which the Federal Reserve and government have declared valuable.

2) There are rules limiting how banks create it, and how *much* they can create.

3) It's possible to produce *fake* e-money, but the hacking knowledge required to do this makes it just as hard as counterfeiting *physical* money.

Password protected

19

Currencies

Money isn't the same everywhere. Each country will usually have its own type of money, called a **currency**. People and businesses from that country will expect to be paid in the local currency.

Clothes, passport... money! Must sort that out.

Sometimes you need to get money in another currency – whether it's for a family trip overseas, or a business making an international deal.

To exchange one currency for another, you need to know how much the currencies cost in relation to each other – this is what's known as an **exchange rate**.

I think I'll need about $100 – but how much is that in euros?

You can exchange different currencies at a business called a foreign exchange bureau. It's also often possible to do this at a bank or post office. These places usually display the relative value of each currency on boards like this:

This board shows how much 1 US dollar is worth in other currencies.

Places that exchange currencies make money by buying them at one rate and selling them on for more.

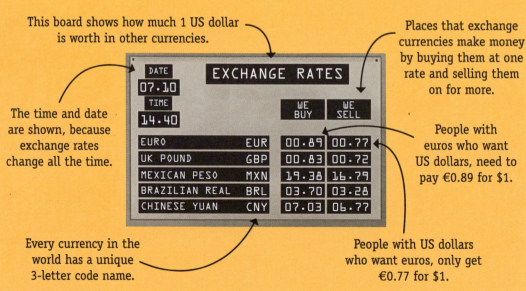

The time and date are shown, because exchange rates change all the time.

People with euros who want US dollars, need to pay €0.89 for $1.

Every currency in the world has a unique 3-letter code name.

People with US dollars who want euros, only get €0.77 for $1.

A currency's value changes all the time, depending on how many people want it – the higher the demand for it, the higher its value.

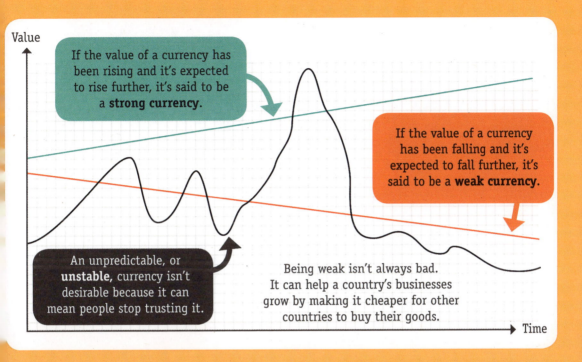

There are several reasons why some currencies are in more demand than others.

Valuing trust

A currency's value depends on how much people trust that country's government. If people don't, the value of that currency will go down.

Strong business

The more business a country does, the higher the demand for its currency.

Political decisions

Governments decide how much new money to create. If they reduce the amount, their currency will become rarer, which may make it more expensive.

If a currency is both strong and stable, it's likely to become a **reserve currency**. This means that banks and governments buy that currency to store their wealth. Today, the world's most dominant reserve currency is the US dollar, but countries also use the euro, UK pound and the Chinese yuan.

21

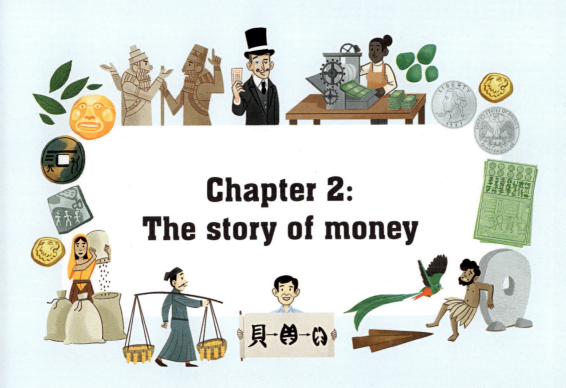

Chapter 2: The story of money

Money has been used for at least as long as people have been able to write things down. We know this because many of the oldest examples of writing are receipts and lists of things people owed each other.

It's likely, however, that some form of money existed long before this – before it even had a name.
As an idea, it seems to have occurred to people all around the world, rather than spreading from one place to another.

But how did it end up in the form it has today?

Not quite money

The oldest surviving evidence of people using money to trade goods comes from Mesopotamia (modern-day Iraq), around 9,000 years ago. Before this, historians think people used a mixture of methods to trade with each other.

In some instances, people had to barter or trade things...

- Hi Ibbi! Can I PLEASE have one of your cows?
- Sure! If you give me four bags of your grain.

...and as we know, bartering only works if both people have what the other wants.

- I have more grain for you. Can I have another cow?
- No thanks Nasha. I've still got some left over... Maybe Kesed can help.

To solve this problem, people bartered with each other until they found something else to trade with.

- Hi Kesed, can I interest you in some of my grain?
- Yes please... I don't have a cow, but I can offer you deer skins?

- I traded my grain for deer skins. Are you interested?
- You bet! Just what I need to keep warm this winter. Here's your cow.

The more people traded, the more they learned about deals *other* people made. Over time, they started to get a sense of how much things were worth.

- The people in the hills will trade two deer skins for only THREE bags of grain.
- But I heard they pay SIX bags for a cow.
- Eeek... I've only got five bags left... I'm going to have to be a bit more careful with my grain from now on.

Sometimes people had the right things to barter with, but they weren't ready at the right times, so they made promises to each other instead. This sort of promise is also known as an **I.O.U.** (short for "I owe you").

Although no one used the word "money" to describe these promises and transactions, all the ingredients of money were there.

Nasha used my deer skins as a *medium of exchange* to trade his grain for Ibbi's cow.

By using bags of grain to measure how much things were worth, we used the grain as a *unit of account*.

Ibbi **trusted** me and so he gave me his cow in exchange for a promise.

Definitely money

We know Mesopotamians used these things as money because they wrote down records of debts they owed each other, and how these debts were paid. This is some of the earliest ever writing. Records show they used a grain called barley to measure small sums, and silver to measure larger amounts. They may have even used barley seeds and slivers of silver as coins – although none survive.

Funny money

At least since Mesopotamian times – and all over the world – people have used a variety of things in the same way we use cash today. These simple forms of money varied wildly...

These forms of money were often desirable in some way, and had their own value.

But many of them also had drawbacks, too.

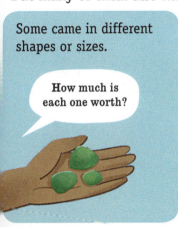

Some forms had fewer drawbacks than others. For instance, cowrie shells were both rare and desirable. They were also **portable**, **durable** and came in a fairly **uniform** size.

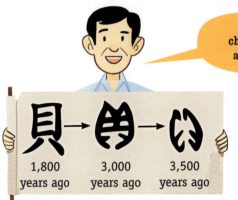

In classical Chinese, the written character for "wealth" (貝) is based on an ancient drawing of a cowrie shell.

In China, cowrie shells were such a successful form of money, people started to make bronze copies to use as well.

Bronze copies were first used around 2,400 years ago. These small, man-made, metal objects had a lot in common with another, much more recognizable form of money that was already being used in China, and beyond – **coins**.

27

The rise of the coin

Money has taken many different forms throughout history, but some things have been used more widely than others. Over time, small flat discs, made from certain metals, especially **gold** and **silver**, came to be used across the globe.

The earliest coins were made in Lydia (modern day Turkey) around 2,700 years ago.

In China, bronze coins like this first appeared around 2,400 years ago.

Coins weren't used in the Americas until European settlers came, but people traded with gold objects.

Not all coins were round – silver coins like this were used in India around 2,400 years ago.

Gold and silver were the perfect materials to make coins – rare enough to be precious, but not *too* rare, so almost anyone could have a little.

Gold and silver were too valuable to use for everyday business, so people also made coins from other, less rare metals, too.

Gold   Silver   Brass   Bronze

In Ancient Rome, a single gold coin held the same value as 25 silver coins, or 200 brass coins, or 1600 bronze coins.

1 gold *aureus*

For most people, one silver coin was worth one day's pay – so one aureus was nearly a month's wage.

25 silver *denarii*

200 brass *dupondius*

1600 bronze *quadrans*

28

Coins were made, or **minted**, by local rulers and governments who used them to collect taxes. They had to be recognizable, so people could feel confident spending them and accepting them. Many features of coins haven't changed since they were first used, around 2,700 years ago.

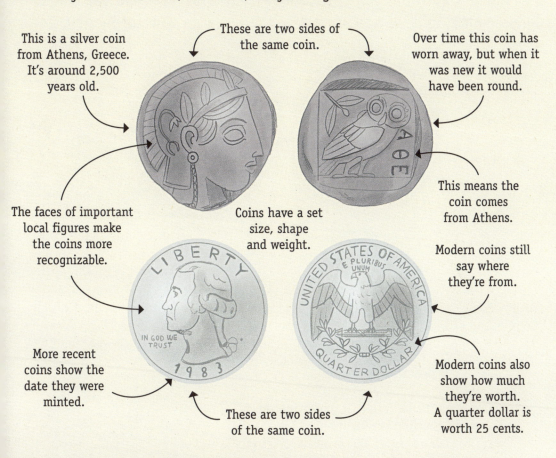

This is a silver coin from Athens, Greece. It's around 2,500 years old.

These are two sides of the same coin.

Over time this coin has worn away, but when it was new it would have been round.

The faces of important local figures make the coins more recognizable.

Coins have a set size, shape and weight.

This means the coin comes from Athens.

Modern coins still say where they're from.

More recent coins show the date they were minted.

These are two sides of the same coin.

Modern coins also show how much they're worth. A quarter dollar is worth 25 cents.

This system worked well for over a thousand years, but coins weren't perfect. They were heavy to carry in big quantities and, worse, people could steal them. People found creative ways to cheat with coins, too.

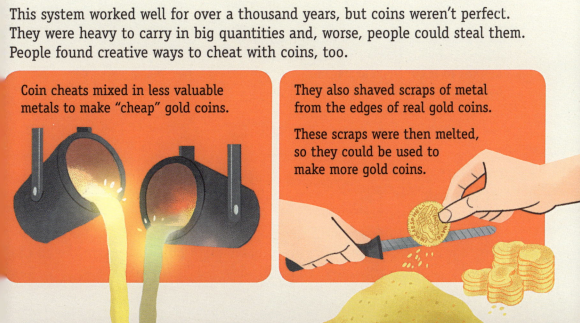

Coin cheats mixed in less valuable metals to make "cheap" gold coins.

They also shaved scraps of metal from the edges of real gold coins.

These scraps were then melted, so they could be used to make more gold coins.

Bills

One of the major problems with coins is that people often needed lots of them to pay for expensive things. Then, around 1,000 years ago, people came up with a new way to handle large sums of money.

Carrying heavy coins around was a pain...

...and it could make you a target for robbers.

To solve this problem, bankers in China offered to store people's coins in secure vaults. They would then issue paper receipts, called *Jiaozi*, to show how much people had stored. Instead of reclaiming their coins, people used these receipts to pay for things – whoever had the receipt could then collect the coins.

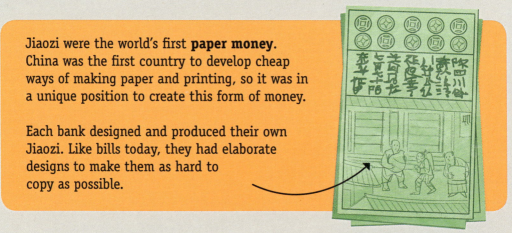

Jiaozi were the world's first **paper money**. China was the first country to develop cheap ways of making paper and printing, so it was in a unique position to create this form of money.

Each bank designed and produced their own Jiaozi. Like bills today, they had elaborate designs to make them as hard to copy as possible.

Jiaozi weren't perfect. They were only ever used to represent really large sums of money, so most people didn't use them. They were easier to copy than coins, too. Banks at this time were risky businesses. If they failed, their customers would be left with worthless receipts for money they couldn't reclaim.

It took a while for this system to catch on. It was even abandoned for around 400 years. But in time, China began printing standard bills that worked in all the major banks – a system that survives to this day.

Not worth the paper it's printed on

Modern bills still look as if they're receipts, just like Jiaozi. In some countries, the signature of the chief banker has been printed next to a sentence that says:

"I promise to pay the bearer on demand the sum of..."

But if you took that bill into a bank to "demand" to be paid, they wouldn't do anything. That's because all money today is fiat money – it isn't linked to a store of coins, or gold, or anything else. Fiat money gets its name from the word *fiat*, which means "let it be done" in Latin – it's only valuable because the government says so. This hasn't always been the case...

I promise to pay the bearer on demand the sum of £20

In 1816, the British government promised to exchange a fixed amount of gold for its currency. This was known as the **gold standard**.

> Should I wish, I could use this bill to claim £10 worth of gold. It's being kept safe in the Bank of England.

In time, the currencies of other countries joined the same standard.

Canada: 1854
Germany, France, USA: 1873
Sweden, Norway, Denmark: 1876
Japan: 1897

When the First World War broke out in 1914, many countries, including Britain, found they needed to spend vast amounts of money.

> Quick, print more bills now! The war won't pay for itself...

Governments discovered they'd printed more money than could be matched by ALL the gold in the world. But they also realized this *didn't matter* – so long as people kept trusting banks.

The gold standard soon became a thing of the past. It ended for good in 1971 when the USA became the last country to stop using it. Bills were no longer linked to anything else. The age of fiat money had begun.

Money in all its forms

Money isn't just about cash or e-money. It is, at heart, a promise that most people trust. Over the centuries, people have developed at least three other ways to turn promises into money.

Debts

...are money that someone promises to pay you in the future.

In this example, Julie and Rob are using debt as money. Instead of paying Rob back in money, Julie has agreed to take on his debt instead.

Debt is often described as something you *have* – when you have debts, you owe money. But it's also something you can *buy*.

When you buy debt, you're owed money by a debtor. This can be valuable because debtors usually pay back an extra fee called interest (see page 60). Buying debt can be risky because debtors aren't always able to pay you back. But if they are reliable, this risk is very low.

One type of low-risk debt that people can buy is called a **bond**. This sort of debt typically lasts a very long time. It's usually sold by governments or big companies who are very likely to be able to repay the money in the future.

Stocks and shares

...are money that you've paid to own a small part of a business.

If you own one or more *stocks*, it means you have a *share* in the business's profits. If the business is doing well, you might get regular payments from it, or you could choose to sell your stocks, hopefully for more than you paid.

Derivatives

...are promises of money based on the value of some other thing, such as a stock, or debt, or just something people produce, such as wheat.

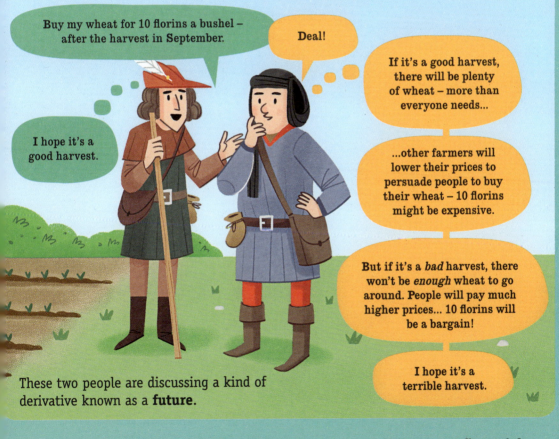

These two people are discussing a kind of derivative known as a **future**.

Debts, stocks, derivatives and other forms of money are all known as **financial instruments.** You can exchange them with other people *as if* they were money. Most people who work in banks – especially the highest paid ones – advise rich customers on how to get even richer by buying and selling financial instruments.

33

Chapter 3:
In the bank

Many people's first experience of banking is storing money in a **piggy bank**. But, as you save more money, you might need to put it in a **commercial bank** instead. This is because commercial banks are safer and more convenient.

But a bank is more than simply a piggy bank for grown-ups. Banks do lots of things that piggy banks can't. They **lend** people money, and to do so they **create** new money out of nothing. If this sounds a little like magic, that's because, in some ways, it *is*.

This chapter looks at what different types of banks do, why and how they do it, and some of the effects they can have on the world.

Where's my money?

Almost all adults put, or **deposit**, their money in a bank. But they rarely think about what happens to that money. This is partly due to misleading language people use when they talk about banks.

In reality, that's *not* what happens. When you deposit money, it becomes part of a big "pool" of deposits and earnings that belong to ALL the branches of that bank.

A large chunk of this money comes from people's deposits, but not all of it. Banks often borrow money from other banks, and they *earn* money by charging people to borrow money from them, too.

Once your money is in the pool, a number of things might happen to it. For example...

It gets spent

A bank is a business. Like all businesses, a bank spends money all the time to pay for the day-to-day running of the bank, and to help it grow and improve.

It's the end of the month. Time to pay staff!

Our website needs a revamp. Let's pay someone to spruce it up.

We're opening a new branch in Japan. We'll need to rent a building.

We need to pay back some of the money we borrowed from another bank.

It gets stored

Banks *don't* need to store the full amount of money that has been deposited. It's very unlikely every customer will **withdraw** all their money at once.

Instead, most banks keep *some* cash in a super-secure vault in the bank...

Extra safe from criminals!

klang

...*some* in another bank, known as the **Federal Reserve**...

Find out more about the Federal Reserve on page 99.

beep

...and the rest in **ATMs***, or **cash machines**, where customers can withdraw it.

But all this cash added together is only 10% of the total money our bank owns. The rest is e-money, stored as numbers on our computers.

*ATM means *Automated Teller Machine.*

37

Why people want banks

Even if you start out keeping money in a jar or **piggy bank**, sooner or later, you'll most likely move it to a bank instead. This kind of bank is known as a **commercial** or **retail** bank.

But why use a bank when you can store cash at home?

Because...

It's safe and secure

Banks keep money safe from criminals. Bank computers are protected – it's extremely difficult for hackers to steal people's details. And the vaults where banks keep cash are very secure too, with security cameras in every room.

You can track it

When you deposit money in a bank, the bank keeps track of how much you spend and how much you have left.
A **bank account** is a record of how much money you have available. There are several different types of accounts.

There are many ways to spend it

When you have a bank account, you can pay for things with a debit card, online or with an app on your phone. You can also use the card to withdraw cash from an ATM.

Your money grows

As you know from the previous page, banks *use* the money you deposit. They may thank you for your deposits (and encourage you to deposit more) by adding money to your account at the end of each month or year. This is known as **interest**. Many people save money for the future this way.

Okay, fair enough. I guess banks have something going for them.

Borrowing money

When people, businesses and governments need money to buy something they can't afford, a bank might agree to lend, or **loan**, them money. People borrow money from the bank for all sorts of reasons.

Banks will only lend you money if they decide they can trust you to pay back the full amount, plus interest. Find out how they decide on page 62.

Why do banks charge interest?

Banks charge interest for lots of reasons. It's the main way they make money. It's also a safety net if things go wrong – interest from successful loans helps make up for money lost on loans that people don't pay back. There's another big reason, too – interest helps stop money from losing value over time. Find out more on pages 98-99.

How banks create money

Another misleading word people use when talking about banks is *lending*. Banks don't actually lend money they *already have* – they **create** the money to lend, as if by magic. Here's how it works.

Zak needs a loan of $50,000 from the bank to start up a business.

After reviewing his application, the bank thinks Zak's business idea will work well. So it agrees to lend him the money.

The bank creates NEW e-money by typing $50,000 into a computer and adding it to Zak's account, while also noting down $50,000 as missing from the bank's own money.

The +$50,000 and the -$50,000 are just numbers on a computer – they cancel each other out with every dollar that Zak pays back, until the bank is missing nothing. But before Zak has to do this, he has $50,000 to spend on his business. He can then use the money the business makes to pay the bank back.

A risky trick?

Around 97% of all the money currently in banks has been created this way. It exists as numbers in people's bank accounts, and debts owed in a bank's own accounts. The rest is cash, created by governments.

But if there's more e-money than cash, what would happen if everyone wanted all of their money at once?

If everybody decided to take out their deposits, it wouldn't be possible. This has never happened on a worldwide scale – most people only take out very small amounts of cash. But it HAS happened to individual banks...

When lots of people withdraw their deposits all at once, it's known as a **bank run**, or **run on the bank**. If a bank runs out of cash, it can no longer function, because it can't pay back its depositors. People lose trust in the bank, so stop depositing money there. That means the bank has almost no money to spend.

Bank runs can be prevented by...

Borrowing cash. If a bank is low on cash, it can borrow it from other banks.

Setting limits. Banks can stop you from taking out more than a certain amount each day.

Insuring deposits. Some governments promise to pay depositors their money if the bank can't. This stops people from worrying as much if banks are low on cash.

41

Other types of banks

Not all commercial banks work the same way. **Islamic banks**, which can be found all over the world, have alternative ways to help people buy things, and still make a profit. One of the main things that's different is how they work with interest.

According to Islam, interest is immoral because it can grow over time. This puts unfair pressure on the borrower.

One of the ways Islamic banks get around charging interest is known as *murabaha*. Here's how it works.

This method means the customer agrees a price with the bank that can't be changed. The bank still gets to make a profit, but there's no interest involved, so the debt can't grow bigger.

Most people trust banks and use them regularly, but some people choose to store and borrow money elsewhere. Here are some common alternatives.

What do these terms mean?

Crowdfunding involves presenting an idea to the public, often on a crowdfunding website. People who think it's a good idea can help to pay for it. In return, you offer these people a reward when the project is finished. For example, in this case, a copy of the movie. If you can't raise enough money, you usually have to give it all back.

Credit unions are like small, simple banks. Instead of customers, they have *members*, who all have a say in how the union is run. If a member wants to borrow money, the union will lend them other members' deposits, and will charge less interest than most banks. In some places, organizations known as **building societies** do this too.

Peer-to-peer lenders are companies that put people who want to *lend* in touch with people who want to *borrow*. Lenders see requests from potential borrowers, and can choose who to lend to. Lenders don't need to charge as much interest as a bank to make a profit, because they don't have extra costs to cover, such as paying staff and running a business.

Offshore banking

When businesses or people earn money, they have to give some of it to the government, as **taxes**. But which government? Some avoid paying taxes by having a bank account in a country where the government doesn't demand much tax. These places are known as **offshore tax havens.**

Denise, a wealthy businesswoman and investor, isn't happy with how much she pays in taxes.

If Denise sets up a shell company, she can open a bank account for it in the tax haven, then make sure money she earns from her investments goes straight to that account. Taxes would be charged on her earnings as if the earnings were made there. In the end, she'd pay *much* less in taxes.

Famous tax havens include the British Virgin Islands in the Caribbean, and the Channel Islands between France and the UK. Tax havens are often heavily criticized. Here are some reasons why.

- Governments worldwide lose around $700 billion in taxes each year.

- If governments had more money from taxes, they'd have more to spend on people in need.

- But businesses and investors help people in need, too. If I have more money to invest, the businesses I invest in have more money to create jobs, or make their products cheaper.

- Hmm... but even if that's true, it's still not fair. If I have to pay taxes, why shouldn't a rich person, or a big business?

- You shouldn't! Personally, I vote for a government that cuts taxes for everybody.

- Well how do you expect governments to fund things like schools and roads then?

- The banks often keep depositors' identities and money activities secret.

- I've heard that some offshore banks don't check where depositors get their money from, or how they spend it.

- That's often true, and it's a good thing. Checking where the money comes from would breach our customers' privacy.

- But if you don't check at all, it makes it easy for criminals to hide stolen money. And terrorists have been known to fund wars and violence through tax havens.

- But that happens so rarely. Is closing the banks going to stop them? And besides, we also help people in danger keep money safe from criminals and terrorists.

- How do you know that it happens rarely if you don't even check?

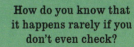

Some researchers have estimated that around 10% of the world's wealth is in tax haven bank accounts. If that was split between everybody in the world, each person would get over $1,000. That's more than people earn in a year in some parts of the world.

Behind-the-scenes banks

There's another kind of bank, known as an **investment bank**, which you're unlikely to come across in your day-to-day life. Most of them are in skyscrapers in big cities, and they do a very important job. They help businesses and governments find funding for really, *really* expensive projects.

Imagine a business called RoboDoc, which makes robots for hospitals. It needs funding to keep growing and to manufacture more robots, but it's not sure where best to get it.

An investment bank might suggest that a business does one of the following things...

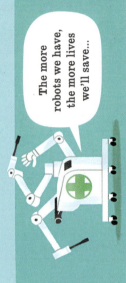

The more robots we have, the more lives we'll save...

Borrow from a bank!

Banks often lend to governments and businesses. The downside: they often charge lots of interest.

Buy another business!

Sometimes businesses go on sale. Buying another business may cost lots of money, but it often means acquiring a bigger team and more resources for making products.

Invest!

It's often possible for a business to make money by using its earnings to buy shares, bonds, derivatives and debts.

Find investors!

This usually means finding people to buy shares in the business. These shares can then be traded with other investors.

JP Investments

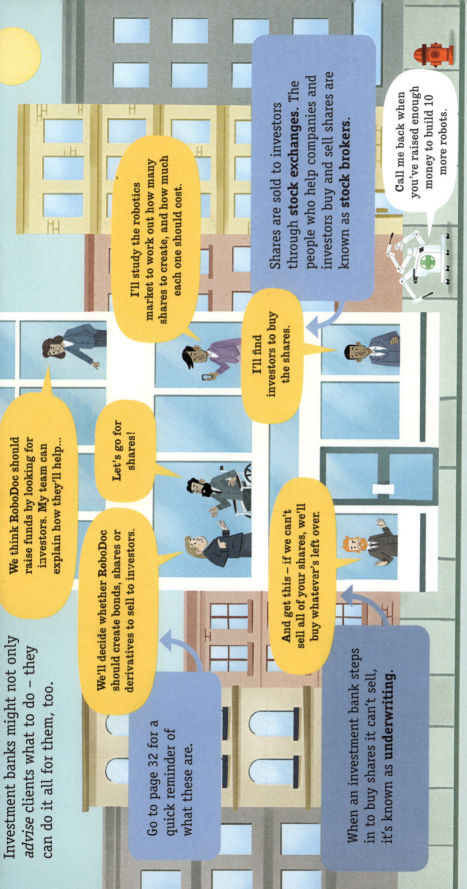

Investment banks might not only *advise* clients what to do – they can do it all for them, too.

We think RoboDoc should raise funds by looking for investors. My team can explain how they'll help...

We'll decide whether RoboDoc should create bonds, shares or derivatives to sell to investors.

Go to page 32 for a quick reminder of what these are.

Let's go for shares!

I'll study the robotics market to work out how many shares to create, and how much each one should cost.

I'll find investors to buy the shares.

Shares are sold to investors through **stock exchanges**. The people who help companies and investors buy and sell shares are known as **stock brokers**.

And get this – if we can't sell all of your shares, we'll buy whatever's left over.

When an investment bank steps in to buy shares it can't sell, it's known as **underwriting**.

Call me back when you've raised enough money to build 10 more robots.

Investment banks are good at these jobs, because they work closely with lots of different companies and investors all the time. They have an excellent overview of who is interested in buying shares, and which shares sell well.
Investment banks charge LOTS of money for this service – hundreds of thousands, or even millions of dollars. But for companies it's often worth it. It would be much harder to find funding for big projects without investment banks.

Banks in crisis

Useful though banks are, they can be dangerous for society if they're run badly. In the years before 2008, commercial and investment banks played a central role in what became a global financial crisis. Here – in short and much simplified – is what happened.

In a bid to make more money, commercial banks in the US began offering mortgages to more and more people. Many of these people were unlikely to be able to pay back the loan and the interest.

The investment banks knew this debt was risky, too, so they bundled up the mortgage repayments with more reliable debt and sold it to investors. This was sometimes illegal.

The banks knew this was risky. If people couldn't pay them back, the banks would lose money. So they *sold* the bad debt to other organizations – usually investment banks.

Now, when borrowers repaid loans, the money went to the investment bank that bought the debt.

Every month, investment banks and investors would share the profit from mortgage repayments. The more people took out mortgages, the more this profit grew.

This system seemed to be working. Houses kept going up in value. People sold their old houses for more than they paid for them, paid off their mortgages, and took out new mortgages on more expensive homes...

...until house prices stopped rising. Many people could no longer pay off mortgages by selling their homes. Huge numbers of people were in debt that they simply couldn't repay.

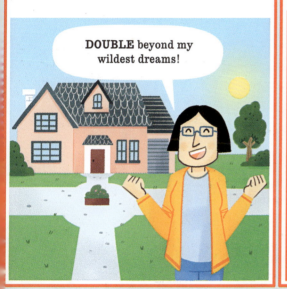

This was a disaster. Commercial banks couldn't sell any debt to investment banks. Investment banks had no repayments to pay to investors. Everybody in the chain was losing money, and losing trust in each other. The consequences were dire.

There was less money around. People lost their jobs, and many couldn't afford basic necessities. When this happens on a large scale over a period of time, it's known as a **recession**. This one was a BIG one.

Banks and investors all over the world were involved, so the recession spread beyond the US to other countries. BILLIONS of people were affected.

Anger at the banks

By mid-2008, some banks had lost SO much money they were forced to shut down. Others stopped lending, which meant people and businesses couldn't borrow. In some places, governments opted to save banks that were close to failing, by giving them LOTS of tax money. People were angry.

Why should **WE** pay for the bankers' foolish, greedy mistakes!

If the banks get saved whenever they behave badly, will they learn a lesson? They'll keep being reckless!

The government didn't rescue **MY** business when it failed. What makes banks so special?

When governments try to save a business by giving it money, it's known as a **bailout**.

BAIL OUT THE PEOPLE, NOT THE BANKS!

Though many people were angry that the bailout happened, not everybody was against it.

I know it doesn't seem fair, but we **NEED** to save the banks, or else businesses will keep on failing. A bailout is the quickest way to do this!

Our taxes aren't just saving the banks, they're saving lots of ordinary people, who rely on banks to borrow money, and to save for when they retire.

Many businesses rely on bank loans to pay staff. If we hadn't acted fast, who knows how many people would have lost their jobs. Society could have collapsed!

Even though the causes of the crisis were unclear, many people directed their anger at the banks and bankers.

> These crooks created the crisis, lied, cheated, and now they get to walk away with a BONUS!?

> WE WANT JUSTICE!

BONUS BANDITS

Despite several top-level bankers breaking the law, only one US banker ended up in jail. It was hard to prove who was responsible for the other crimes.

Some bankers kept large amounts of the bailout money for themselves, instead of using it to reverse the crisis.

CHANGE THE RULES!

Sharing the blame

In reality, not ALL bankers were to blame for the crisis. It was mostly down to a few top-level commercial and investment bankers, who took huge risks. They took those risks because, well, they could.

To prevent another crisis, many governments have set new rules to force bankers to take fewer risks.

The US government is responsible for the crisis, too! THEY set the rules on what US banks can and can't do. They gave the banks too much freedom!

Will history repeat?

Probably, but nobody knows for sure when or how. The UK central bank's website says: "History shows that there are two things we can be sure of when it comes to financial crises: there will be another one, and the next one won't be the same as the last."

Understanding how banks work, and monitoring what they do, can make it less likely there will be another crisis as big as the 2008 financial crisis.

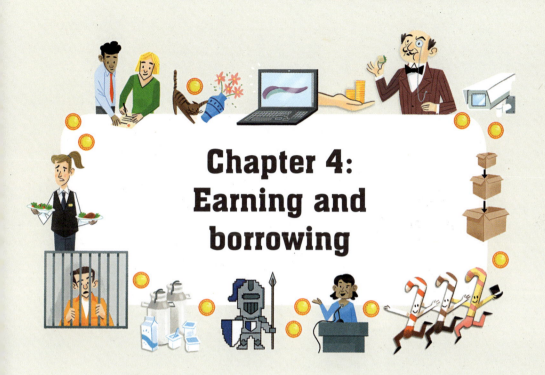

Chapter 4: Earning and borrowing

Have you ever wanted to buy something that you couldn't afford? There are two common solutions to this problem: **earn** some money, or **borrow** some.

There are literally millions of jobs you could do to earn a living, and they would all earn you different amounts. But even people who earn lots and lots have to borrow money from time to time. So many things wouldn't be possible without borrowing, such as buying a house or starting a business.

Earning your way

When you're a child or teenager, you might be given an allowance. But once you grow up, you'll probably need to *earn* money by doing a job that somebody pays you for.

Some jobs are more common... ...and others are more unusual.

There's more than one way for teachers, bus drivers, sandwich tasters and cat trainers to set up their work lives. For example...

Cat trainer Kayla is an **employee** at a cat training company. She...

...is paid an agreed amount of money every month, known as a **salary**.

...gets some paid time off each year, but has to work the same number of hours each week.

...is guaranteed to be paid money, as long as she works for her employer.

Cat trainer Nico is **self-employed**, or **freelance**. People (his **clients**) pay him to do one-off jobs caring for their cats. He...

...earns different amounts every month, depending on how much work he does.

...is not guaranteed paid work. He has to find clients.

...doesn't get paid time off, but can decide how many days and hours he works.

...can register as a **business** and pay employees to work for him.

The job hunt

Most people try to find a job that will pay them enough money to live on. But this isn't the only thing people think about when they look for a job.

I love to travel, so I became a flight attendant. I go to different parts of the world every week, and get paid for it. Bingo!

I'm a freelance website designer. I trained as a programmer, so I have the right skills. And being freelance means I can make time to pick my kids up from school.

I'm a politician – I'm ambitious and wanted a job where I could improve the way this country is run.

As well as offering a monthly or weekly wage, many **employers** offer their **employees** other perks, known as a benefits package.

SAMPLE BENEFITS PACKAGE

- Paid time off.
- Paid medical insurance.
- Paid dental insurance.
- Annual bonus for hitting certain work targets.
- Opportunity to buy shares in the business with company matching contribution.
- Bonus for long service after 10 years.

If you're doing well in your job, you can ask your employee for a raise in your salary. This is known as **negotiating** – you'll find some tips for this on page 118.

High pay, low pay

Some people are paid more than others, whether it seems fair or not. For example, professional soccer players are usually paid much more than gardeners. This is because salaries are partly influenced by how rare a person's skills are – the **supply** – compared to how many employers want those skills – the **demand**. Here's how it happens.

Like anybody with a job, gardeners and soccer pros are paid to provide skills that their employers need.

But some skills are harder than others, so fewer people can do them.

The number of people with top-class soccer skills is low, but there are lots of teams that want those skills, so teams compete for players.

In contrast, the number of people who can grow vegetables is higher than the number of gardeners needed, so gardeners compete for employers.

How low does it go?

To protect workers, many governments have made it illegal for employers to pay employees less than a particular amount. This is known as the **minimum wage**. The minimum wage tends to be smaller in countries where basics such as food and clothes cost very little.

For example, in Israel, bread costs...
$2.17

The minimum wage is $1,446 per month.

In Albania, bread costs...
$0.64

The minimum wage is $212 per month.

Economists and politicians often disagree on how effective a minimum wage really is at protecting citizens.

On the one hand...  On the other hand...

Thank goodness for minimum wages! I'd be living in poverty if my employers paid me any less.

In my city, a minimum wage was introduced. Lots of companies had to stop employing new people because they couldn't afford to keep hiring. Now I can't find a job.

Many employers pay more than the minimum wage, because they believe they'll attract better staff by paying more. But sometimes employees have to campaign to get better pay. Here are some ways they might go about it.

Join a union

Labor unions are groups of workers. They campaign for workers' rights and organize protests known as strikes to encourage employers to improve pay, working conditions or overall fairness.

Tell the media

For example, if a woman is paid less than a man for doing the same job, she might tell a newspaper. Public embarrassment can make employers change their ways.

A helping hand

There are many different ways you can **borrow** money from a bank or lending company. Each way is suited to a different situation where people need money that they don't yet have.

Borrowing small amounts

If somebody needs money to make a quick purchase before they can afford it, they might use a **credit card**.

How it works: a credit card company or a bank pays for your purchase. You then pay them back later – usually within 30 days.

If you don't pay back on time, the bank or company charges **interest**, so the amount you owe goes up.

Some banks will allow you to spend more money than you have in your account, known as having a **line of credit**. But this is nothing more than a loan, and you still have to pay it back. If you spend more than you have in your account, you are said to be **overdrawn** – which can often be very expensive to pay back.

Borrowing large amounts

Imagine two people come across a large, empty warehouse that nobody is using...

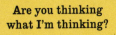

"Are you thinking what I'm thinking?"

"That this would be the perfect place to open a chocolate factory?"

"You read my mind."

But they don't have enough money in the bank to rent the warehouse, buy chocolate-making machines, and pay staff. So they'll have to apply for a **loan** at a bank or lending company.

One week later...

"We want to open a chocolate factory. We've worked out a five-year business plan, but we need money to get started."

"Delicious! Let me see what we can do..."

The lender usually carries out checks to see if the borrower can be trusted to pay back the loan, plus interest.

If the lender says yes, the borrower and lender have to sign a contract, which states...

...how much is being borrowed.

...a deadline for the borrower to pay it all back.

...how much interest is charged. (See next page for more about interest.)

"What if something happens that means we definitely can't pay you back?"

"We get all the machines in your factory. And any leftover chocolate."

"Yikes."

People sometimes give the lender their personal belongings if they don't have money. This is known as **paying with collateral**.

Paying for money

Usually, when you borrow money, you have to pay interest. The amount depends on something known as the **interest rate**, which is a percentage of the amount you borrowed. Here's a simplified example of how it might work.

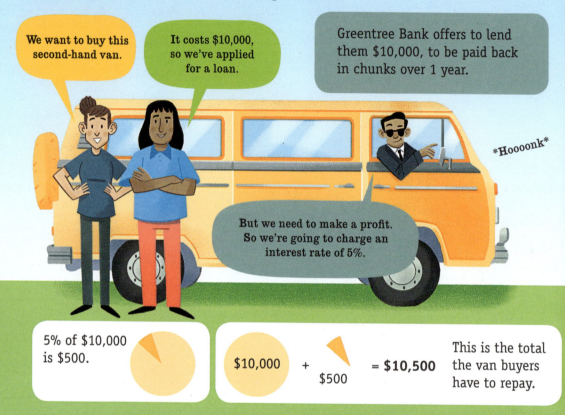

With this kind of loan, you only *fully* own what you've bought once you've paid it *all* back, including the interest (but you can use it in the meantime).

It can take decades to pay back loans. This is partly because some loans (for example to buy a house) are very big, but also because banks like long loans. Long loans with regular repayments mean they have a steady stream of money coming in.

Interest that grows

Most people pay off debts in regular, monthly chunks, including a bit of interest each time. If you delay or miss a payment, you can sometimes end up owing much more than you started with. That's because you have to pay off interest on the part of interest you *didn't* pay. Each month you leave the debt unpaid, the more the interest goes up.

It's a lot like the way a snowball gets bigger more quickly the longer you roll it. For example...

At the end of a month, Ella owes a credit card company $5,000, plus 10% interest.

10% of $5,000 is **$500**, so she owes $5,500.

If she doesn't pay any back by the end of the next month, 10% is added to $5,500.

10% of $5,500 is **$550**, so she now owes $6,050.

The amount the interest increases by gets bigger and bigger each month.

This is known as **compound interest**.

Compound interest can be a terrible thing if it grows for too long – people end up owing very large amounts.

But it can be a good thing too. Most savings accounts *pay* compound interest. So if you leave money in a savings account and don't touch it, your savings will get bigger and bigger, by more and more each year.

German-born scientist and thinker Albert Einstein is supposed to have said about compound interest...

He who understands it, earns it; he who doesn't, pays it.

61

Credit ratings

Most banks and loan companies won't lend money to *everybody* who asks, because some people might not pay it all back. Lenders use a scoring system called a **credit rating** to estimate how risky it is to give somebody a loan.

This flow chart shows some of the things that affect a person's score, and what it means for their borrowing.

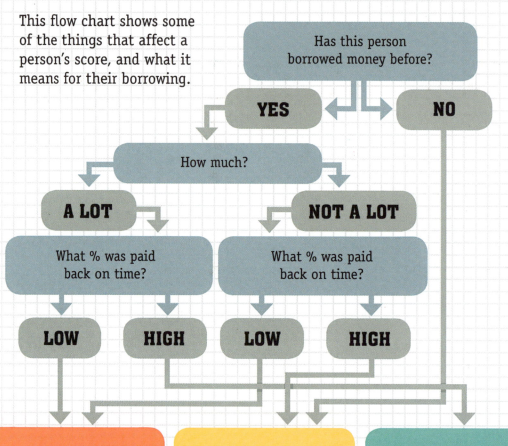

Low score

OFFER: A small loan with high interest and an extra borrowing fee, to make up for the risk that the person might not pay everything back.

Medium score

OFFER: A medium-sized loan with a medium-high interest rate. The person's track record isn't bad, but they don't have much experience of borrowing.

High score

OFFER: A large loan with low interest, meaning low monthly repayments. Lenders trust the loan will be paid back, so they charge less.

A person's score might also be affected by how much debt they're already in, and how regularly they pay their rent or any other bills on time.

Banks support credit ratings, because it helps them decide who to lend money to. But some people are against the system, because it makes it easier for wealthy people to get more money, and it can make it harder for poor people.

If you have a *very* low score, a bank might refuse to lend to you at all. Low scorers sometimes turn to illegal lenders, known as **loan sharks**, who don't worry about credit ratings. This is a bad idea, for many reasons. Here are some of them.

VERY high interest

Loan sharks often charge such a high interest rate that some people are never able to pay the loan back.

My $500 loan ballooned to over $15,000 to pay back, just because of interest!

Pressure

If the interest is too high to repay the loan, some loan sharks persuade people to take out *another* loan to pay off the first, often with an *even* higher interest rate.

Intimidation

Loan sharks have been known to turn up at people's homes to threaten them. They can even be violent if you can't pay them back.

Managing debts

When people borrow money, they usually manage to pay it back – eventually. But unexpected things can happen to anyone, and sometimes debt can spiral out of control. However, even when debt starts to feel unmanageable, there *are* ways out.

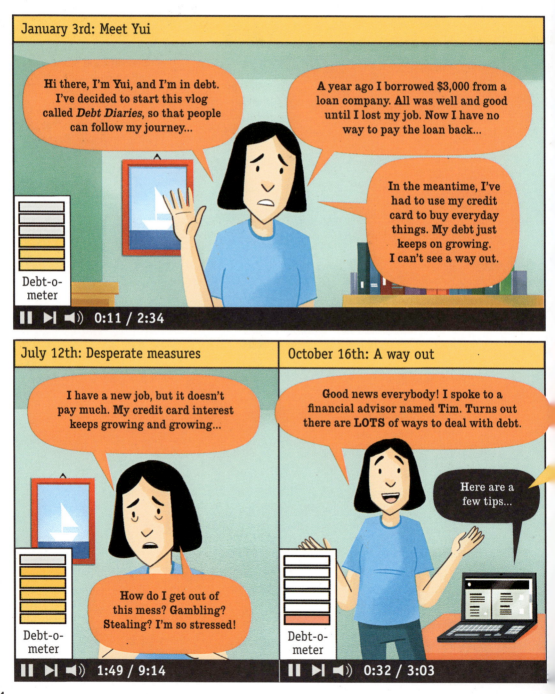

Fri 09:37

http://www.tims-money-tips.com/

TIM'S
MONEY TIPS

"With over 20 years of professional experience, I'm the one to trust when it comes to managing your money!"

Less for longer

Talk to the lender to see if you can pay back in smaller chunks over a longer time.

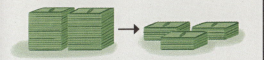

Freeze the debt

Lenders always want their money back, but they're sometimes happy to wait. Ask for a break in repayments for a month or two.

Package it up

Some people owe things to many people and companies at the same time. It can all be a bit confusing. One option is to take out one big loan to pay off those debts, so it's easier to manage.

Write it off

If there's no way you can pay lenders back, some of them might let you off part of your debt. They'd rather have some money than none. This is known as *writing off* debt.

Ask for help

In some places, local governments might also give money to people with unmanageable debt problems.

And I'll be there to guide you along the way.

A last resort

If somebody is in lots and lots of debt and there's no way they can pay it all back, they might apply for **bankruptcy**. This means all their debt is written off. It's a last resort, because even though it takes away some stress, people often have to pay off what they can in collateral. Going bankrupt limits how much you can borrow in the future, and in some places, it even limits the sorts of jobs you can do.

Illegal earning

Money is often at the heart of a crime, whether it's pickpocketing or lying about income to avoid paying taxes. Here are a few examples of ways people try to steal money – sometimes successfully.

Theft

Theft is when you take something from somebody without their permission, often using force. For example, a bank robbery.

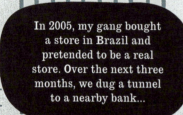

In 2005, my gang bought a store in Brazil and pretended to be a real store. Over the next three months, we dug a tunnel to a nearby bank...

...then we drilled up into the bank's vaults and stole over three tons of Brazilian money.

Fraud

Fraud is when a criminal tricks somebody into giving them money, or into letting them use money they got their hands on illegally.

For example, **embezzlement** is when somebody uses money that a business has given them control over for their own personal gain.

I was in charge of paying people's salaries for a medical charity.

I paid myself $465,000 extra and no one noticed for over 30 years.

Money laundering is a type of fraud, too. It's when somebody disguises where their money came from to make it look as if they got it legally.

I set up a load of fake companies and opened bank accounts in their names.

Then I stole money and paid it to those accounts. It looked as if the businesses had earned real money.

Phishing is when somebody tries to get money or sensitive information, such as people's bank account details, often by sending links to fake websites.

In 2017, staff at a Canadian university were sent emails claiming that a company it owed money to had new bank account details.

The emails *looked* genuine.

The company seemed plausible.

They paid over $8 million into the account, which turned out to belong to a fraudster, not an actual company.

We've been much more careful since this happened.

Card fraud means illegally obtaining and using somebody else's debit or credit card details to take their money, or to sell the card details to others.

In 2007, two men in London installed hidden cameras by ATMs so that they could collect card details from people using the ATMs, including their passwords. They managed to collect the details of over 19,000 people.

Then we printed fake credit cards in a factory and used them to withdraw cash and pay for things. We stole over $20 million in total.

And we nearly got away with it – grr!

67

Protecting money online

The tricks, scams and thefts that happen in real life take place online too. So it's worth being careful about any purchases you might make online and the kind of information you share.

Here are some ways businesses can tempt you into spending money online.

Free trials
Lots of websites and apps offer to let you try their product for free. But all free trials end, and often automatically start charging you.

"Virtual" money
When you buy things with "virtual" money inside a game world, it sometimes actually costs you real money too.

Expensive add-ons
Some games and apps are free up to a point, but then charge you to get to a new level, or for certain features.

It might be dishonest to trick you into overspending like this, but it's not against the law. However, it *is* illegal to trick you into sharing personal information. This is **phishing**, and it can allow someone else to pretend to be you, and spend your money. Here are some of the forms it can take.

An official website
Hackers can make identical copies of official websites, in order to trick people into handing over their login and credit card details.

A suspicious website
A web address in a format you don't recognize

Requests for personal details

A pop-up

Clicking on "OK" here will cause harmful software to download.

A link in a message
Links in text messages or emails can lead you to a webpage that asks for your details.

68

Safety tips

Of course not all links and pop-ups are malicious, but it's not always easy to tell. Here are some tips to avoid getting tricked.

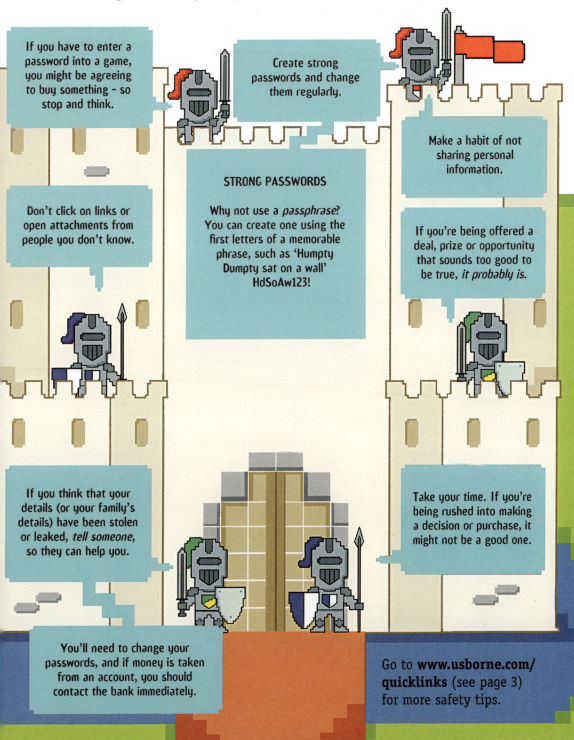

If you have to enter a password into a game, you might be agreeing to buy something – so stop and think.

Create strong passwords and change them regularly.

Make a habit of not sharing personal information.

STRONG PASSWORDS

Why not use a *passphrase*? You can create one using the first letters of a memorable phrase, such as 'Humpty Dumpty sat on a wall' HdSoAw123!

Don't click on links or open attachments from people you don't know.

If you're being offered a deal, prize or opportunity that sounds too good to be true, *it probably is*.

If you think that your details (or your family's details) have been stolen or leaked, *tell someone*, so they can help you.

Take your time. If you're being rushed into making a decision or purchase, it might not be a good one.

You'll need to change your passwords, and if money is taken from an account, you should contact the bank immediately.

Go to **www.usborne.com/ quicklinks** (see page 3) for more safety tips.

69

Chapter 5: Spending, growing and giving

Once you have some money, you can start **spending** it – hooray! But before you rush off and spend it all, it's useful to know how to **manage** your spending. It's easy to fall into a habit of spending too much, and this can make your life very tricky.

It's often wise not to spend *all* of your money. Instead, by **saving** and **investing** you might be able to grow your money into *more* money. Or, you could use your money to help other people, by **donating** it to a cause that you support.

Budgeting

No matter how much money you have or will earn, it's a good idea to plan what you're going to do with it. One way to do this is to write a list of where your money comes from, and how you plan to spend it. This is known as **budgeting**. Here's an example.

Monthly finances

Income:

Salary from job	$3,600.00
Clothes sold online	$120.00
TOTAL	$3,720.00

Expenses:

	Aim to spend	Actually spend
Taxes due	$900.00	$900.00
Rent + bills	$1,020.00	$1,020.00
Transportation	$260.00	$250.00
Food	$200.00	$300.00
Leisure	$940.00	$830.00
Savings	$400.00	$400.00
TOTAL	$3,720.00	$3,700.00

- Some people budget weekly, or every few months.
- **Money in** (and where it comes from)
- An extra way to earn money outside of work
- **Money out** (and where it goes)
- A list of your spending goals is known as your **budget**.
- A list of what you end up spending is known as your **accounts**.

This person stuck to their budget – their income was bigger than their expenses. When people overspend, it means their expenses are bigger than their income.

Keeping track of spending is important. It helps you work out whether you're likely to stick to your budget.

"I'm old-school. I collect receipts and write them up every week."

"My bank account and card connect to an app that logs payments automatically."

Spending wisely

To stick to a budget you usually have to limit your spending. Most people can't afford to buy everything they want, whenever they want it. Here are some tips on how to spend wisely and spend less.

THE DAILY SAVER
May 27th, 2019
99 cents

Ms. Piggybank's spending secrets

Buy out of season

Coats and scarves are cheaper in summer. Buy things well before you (and everybody else) will need them.

But maybe wait to use them...

Comparison shop

Look in several stores and browse online to see if anywhere sells what you want cheaper than other places.

Shop with a list

Many purchases people make are unplanned. That's not always a bad thing. But if it happens all the time, your spending can rocket. Plan your purchases in advance and limit your impulse buys.

If it isn't on the list, it isn't in the cart.

Discount codes

Some websites offer discount codes for when you shop online. Always search for discount codes before you buy.

Walk, walk, walk

If you can get somewhere safely and quickly without hopping in your car, why not save on gas by walking instead?

73

Overspending

Even if you budget carefully, it's still easy to spend more than you planned.

Sometimes people overspend because they have to.

"Gah, my car broke down and the repairs cost a fortune."

"My sister got robbed last month and it's costing her *thousands* to replace everything."

Other times, people spend too much money carelessly, and businesses often encourage them to do so. Here are some of the ways they do it.

Special offers make people more likely to buy things.

Businesses place **advertising** almost anywhere to tempt customers to buy products.

Some companies post glowing but **fake reviews** of their products online.

Others offer customers **discounts**, sometimes just for posting a positive review.

74

Expensive accidents

Often when people have to make large payments, it's because something unexpected has happened. Luckily, it's sometimes possible to get *somebody else* to cover the cost of repairs and replacements. This is the world of **insurance**.

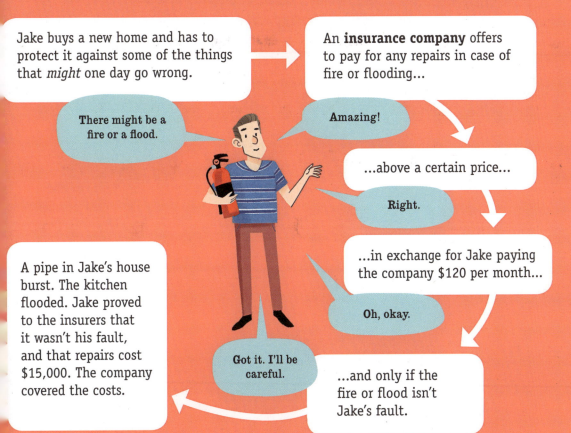

Jake buys a new home and has to protect it against some of the things that *might* one day go wrong.

There might be a fire or a flood.

An **insurance company** offers to pay for any repairs in case of fire or flooding...

Amazing!

...above a certain price...

Right.

...in exchange for Jake paying the company $120 per month...

Oh, okay.

...and only if the fire or flood isn't Jake's fault.

Got it. I'll be careful.

A pipe in Jake's house burst. The kitchen flooded. Jake proved to the insurers that it wasn't his fault, and that repairs cost $15,000. The company covered the costs.

People can buy insurance to cover the costs of almost anything unplanned.

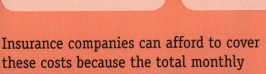

Missing a flight   A sick pet   Tripping

Insurance companies can afford to cover these costs because the total monthly payments from all their customers come to more than the amount they spend on things going wrong. But most try to avoid covering costs, by making it hard to prove the accident *wasn't* your fault.

Sorry sir, we won't pay to replace what was stolen. You posted on social media that you were on vacation. The burglars might have seen your post and known you weren't home.

75

Growing money in a bank

Money isn't just for spending. You can use it to make even more money. One way to do this is by depositing it in a bank account that earns interest. It's a handy way of earning a bit more and saving for the future. Here's how it works.

If you've read chapter 3, you'll know that your money doesn't just sit in a bank account doing nothing...

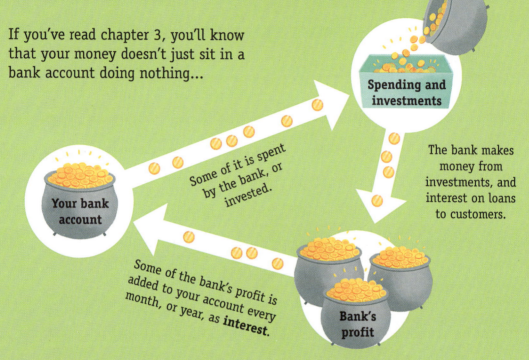

Some of it is spent by the bank, or invested.

The bank makes money from investments, and interest on loans to customers.

Some of the bank's profit is added to your account every month, or year, as **interest**.

The amount of interest you receive is a percentage of the money in your account. This is known as an **interest rate**. Different types of accounts have different interest rates. If you don't spend your money, it will grow by different amounts, depending on the type of account you put it in.

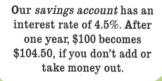

Our *savings account* has an interest rate of 4.5%. After one year, $100 becomes $104.50, if you don't add or take money out.

Our *checking account* doesn't earn any interest. After one year, $100 will still be $100, if you don't add or take money out.

GREEN TREE BANKING

Checking accounts tend to have lower interest rates than savings accounts. Why?

Checking accounts are designed to make everyday spending easier.

I can access my money immediately using a debit card.

I can pay for stuff online.

And I can take out my money whenever I want.

Most people use their checking account several times each week, so the amount in the account changes often.

Savings accounts are designed to help people save and grow their money.

I can only access my money by transferring it into my checking account, or by going to the bank directly.

And I can only transfer money a limited number of times each month.

It's harder to use money in a savings account to pay for things, so the amount in the account changes quite rarely.

Banks need *reliable* sources of money so that they know how much they can lend out or invest.

The amount in savings accounts changes less than checking accounts, making savings accounts more reliable. So banks try to encourage people to open them by offering higher interest rates.

Who doesn't want to see their money grow fast?

Growing money by investing

Another way of "growing" money is by **investing** – spending money on something, hoping to make a profit from it later. Anything you buy or own that can you sell on is known as an **asset**. Here are three examples of assets that Reena could invest in...

Precious things

Some expensive things can become even more expensive over time, such as houses, artwork, or precious objects. But it's never guaranteed.

Selling an asset in the future – if it's worth more – will make Reena a profit.

Bonds

Bonds are debts you buy from companies or governments (see page 32).

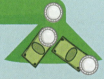

The company or government promises to pay the debt back by an agreed date (usually years in the future) *plus interest*.

Shares

A **share** is a small part of a company (see page 33).

If a company does well, the value of its shares goes up...

...sometimes very quickly.

Reena might make money from shares in two ways.

1. Selling her shares for more than she paid – usually when the company is doing well.

2. Receiving regular payments from the company's profits, known as **dividends**.

> But I could **LOSE** money, too. If the value of my shares drops by too much, I might not be able to sell them for more than I paid.

Earning without working

A few people are able to invest enough money to make a large regular income from their investments – even after they've paid taxes on it. Twenty years later, Reena has continued to invest and save, and now she wants to stop working.

She has...

...$500,000 invested in shares, which earns her $19,000 a year.

...$1,000,000 in a savings account, which earns her $40,000 interest a year.

...two apartments that people rent from her, which earn her $20,000 a year.

$79,000 a year? Fit for a queen.

Most people will never earn enough to make all these investments. But even people with a little wealth can *gradually* invest more over many, many years. With a lot of time, effort, and a little luck, they might make enough from their investments to stop working, like Reena.

A note of caution

Investments can be risky and they're never *guaranteed* to keep making money.

For example, a business you have shares in might fail and stop paying dividends, or the interest on your savings account might drop.

Over time, prices tend to rise due to a process known as **inflation** (find out more on page 98).

As prices rise, your money buys you less. In ten years' time, $79,000 might be worth much less than it is now.

Back in my day, $1 would buy me a ticket to a pro ball game. Now it won't even buy me a hot dog!

Buying and selling shares

Most bonds and shares are traded by people known as **stockbrokers** through places known as **stock exchanges**. Companies and investors tell stockbrokers how many shares or bonds they want to *sell*. Other investors then negotiate a price with the brokers before *buying*.

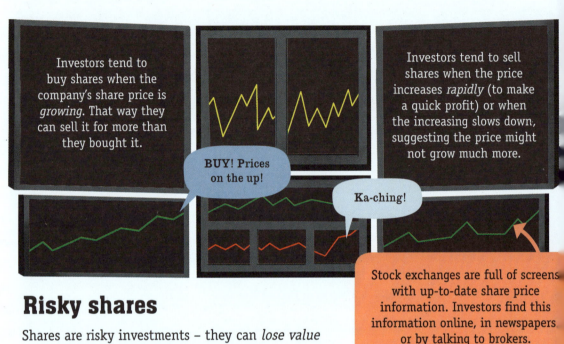

Investors tend to buy shares when the company's share price is *growing*. That way they can sell it for more than they bought it.

BUY! Prices on the up!

Ka-ching!

Investors tend to sell shares when the price increases *rapidly* (to make a quick profit) or when the increasing slows down, suggesting the price might not grow much more.

Stock exchanges are full of screens with up-to-date share price information. Investors find this information online, in newspapers or by talking to brokers.

Risky shares

Shares are risky investments – they can *lose value* just as quickly as they *gain value*. Reena has shares in *Sunny Juice Corporation* and keeps an eye on them. She talks to her stockbroker when she has questions.

Yikes! Shares prices have suddenly dropped... What now?

Want to chat?

LIVECHAT with ShareCo.

Hi, share prices in *Sunny Juice Co.* have plummeted. Should I sell mine before the price drops more?

Give it a few more days. The price will probably start rising again.

Okay. What if it keeps falling?

Sell, so you don't lose your money, then buy shares in *Lumbar Rice* — they're going up.

Another way Reena could minimize risk is by spreading her investments across lots of companies.

That way, if one company's share price starts dropping, but the others rise or stay the same, her losses won't be too huge. This is called **diversifying**. Reena can diversify on her own, or she can invest in a **mutual fund** – a company that diversifies *for her* and takes part of the money those investments earn.

Good shares, bad shares

Some people think certain investments are harmful. Others disagree.

Raising money for a cause

You don't have to be rich to give money to a good cause. People often raise money for charity by organizing events or activities that people can pay to take part in. This is known as **fundraising**.

Fundraising is hard work, and it's a good idea to get help. You could start by asking a family member or a teacher. Then use the questions and tips below to plan your event.

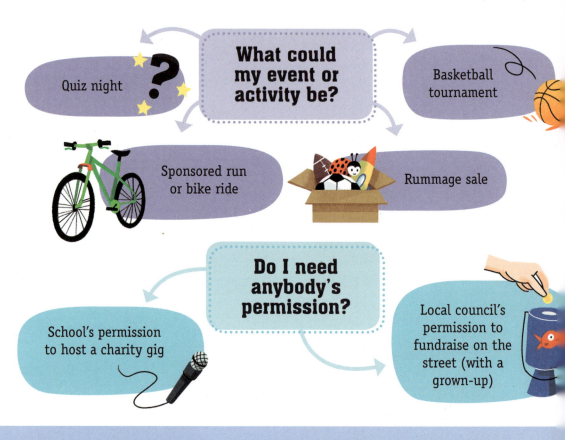

Tips and tricks

There are lots of fundraising techniques that make people more likely to donate. Here are just a few, with examples of how you might use them to raise money for a stray dog charity.

Have a clear target.

Let's raise $500 for our local stray dog charity!

Give incentives.

If you donate $8, I'll walk your dog EVERY DAY for a week.

Advertise in the local newspaper?

Make posters?

How can I spread the word about my event?

Announcement in school assembly?

Create event on social media?

Set up a crowdfunding website (see page 43)?

Paying to rent a room (for example for a trivia night)?

Buying materials (such as snacks for the basketball teams)?

What costs might there be? Make sure you raise more than you spend.

Invitations and thank you notes?

Promotional materials to let people know about your event?

Emotional stories are often more persuasive than facts and figures.

Have multiple ways to donate and share the information.

This is how lonely Sniffles found a loving home...

Every year, 100,000 stray dogs end up in shelters...

If you can't come along but want to donate and tell your friends, visit the charity's website, click donate, and send the link to everyone you know!

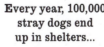
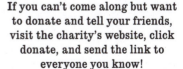

83

Choosing a cause

Is it more important to protect animals or provide people in dry parts of the world with fresh water? There are so many charities out there that need donations. How do you choose one over any other?

There's no right or wrong answer to the question, "Is one charity better than another?" There are many different reasons to donate to a charity, including its relevance to you and how effective your donation would be.

Philanthropy

For very wealthy people, donating large one-off amounts isn't always the most effective way to use money for good. Instead, setting up organizations known as **philanthropic foundations** allows them to make large, *regular* donations to good causes.

Philanthropic foundations are largely funded by the money that grows from a wealthy person's investments.

I invested **BILLIONS** in shares and properties.

Azim Premji, Indian businessman and philanthropist

Then I set up a foundation that uses money from those investments to open schools in rural parts of India.

The money that grows from investments provides a large, regular source of funding. That means foundations (and any institutions that foundations fund) have a reliable income, so they can keep on doing their work for a long time.

Often much longer than the people who founded them!

A. CARNEGIE
1835 - 1919

The foundations set up by Scottish-born businessman Andrew Carnegie still help fund hundreds of libraries around the world. He helped set up those libraries with the vast fortune he made in the steel industry.

Is giving always good?

Charities and foundations play vital roles in improving people's lives worldwide. But not everybody agrees that *all* types of philanthropy and donations are good. Here are some reasons why.

Some people prefer to donate to charities and foundations that help solve the *causes* of a problem, not just the *effects*.

"Donate to help us clean plastic from the oceans!"

"Shouldn't you be stopping the plastic from getting there in the first place?"

Some people think you should only donate money to the poorest and most disadvantaged in the world.

"A wealthy university doesn't need more money!"

"It does! We're using it to develop solutions to big problems that will benefit everybody, such as vaccines to prevent deadly diseases."

Funding for foundations can come from profits from investments in companies that exploit people.

Some people say that companies should spend charitable money on running their own company more fairly, rather than giving money away to other causes.

"The fashion company I invest in pays **HUGE** dividends. I could use that money to help find a cure for cancer."

"But what about the people who make the clothes? We're overworked and underpaid!"

Giving money isn't as simple as "always good" or "always bad." There are different ways to give, and different organizations to donate to. It's a good idea to research each option before giving money, to decide which you think will help most.

Chapter 6: Governments and money

Money doesn't just move between banks, businesses and people – it's also used by governments. They get LOTS of it from taxes – often billions, if not *trillions*, of dollars. Then they spend this money on **public services** such as schools, roads and the police.

One of the main jobs for every government is to decide how to manage **taxpayers'** money. Even small choices have big consequences – if a government closes a library or builds a playground, it won't make much difference to the total amount it spends, but it can have a huge impact on people's day-to-day lives.

How taxes work

Almost everybody in every country has to pay some taxes. Most governments set out to collect them in a fair way, but people often disagree about what it means to be fair.

Types of taxes

Throughout history, governments have charged taxes on many things. For instance, around 300 years ago, men in Russia had to pay taxes if they had beards. Today, the sorts of taxes people pay don't vary much from country to country. Here are some of the main types, but they're not all used everywhere.

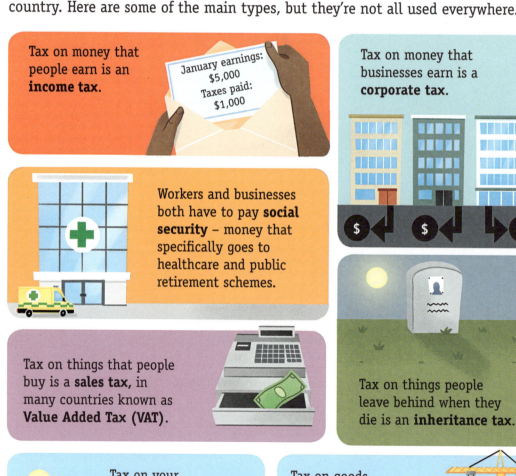

Tax on money that people earn is an **income tax**.

January earnings: $5,000
Taxes paid: $1,000

Tax on money that businesses earn is a **corporate tax**.

Workers and businesses both have to pay **social security** – money that specifically goes to healthcare and public retirement schemes.

Tax on things that people buy is a **sales tax**, in many countries known as **Value Added Tax (VAT)**.

Tax on things people leave behind when they die is an **inheritance tax**.

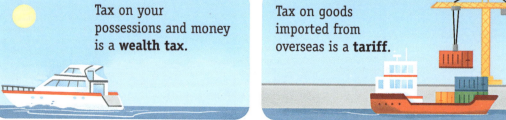

Tax on your possessions and money is a **wealth tax**.

Tax on goods imported from overseas is a **tariff**.

Making taxes fair

Taxes are often calculated as a percentage of the total value of something, such as your income. This percentage is called the **tax rate**, and it's designed to make the tax system fairer.

Governments often set higher tax rates for higher earners. This is called a **progressive tax** because the tax rate *progresses*, or increases, as people earn more.

Progressive taxes are meant to make society fairer by taking money from the rich and spending it on things that mostly help the poor.

It might seem unfair to tax people different amounts, but imagine if everyone paid $10,000 a year instead...

Hmm, it's a pretty steep tax rate for me. I only earn $20,000 a year, so $10,000 is 50% of my wages.

It's much better for me. I earn $200,000 a year, so $10,000 is only 5% of my wages.

When governments tax everyone the same amount, it's called a **regressive tax** because the rate *regresses*, or decreases, as people earn more.

Taxes and choices

Often governments use taxes to change the way people spend their money.

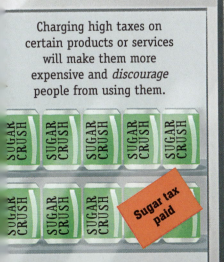

Charging high taxes on certain products or services will make them more expensive and *discourage* people from using them.

Charging low taxes on products or services will make them cheaper and *encourage* more people to use them. This is what's known as a **tax break**.

Tariffs discourage people from buying foreign goods and encourage people to trade within their own country.

Spending public money

Governments use money from taxes to pay for jobs and services that many people take for granted. If they didn't, we'd have to organize these things ourselves. It's up to each government to decide how much it can afford to spend and what services it should provide.

Here are some examples of what a government might buy with money from taxes.

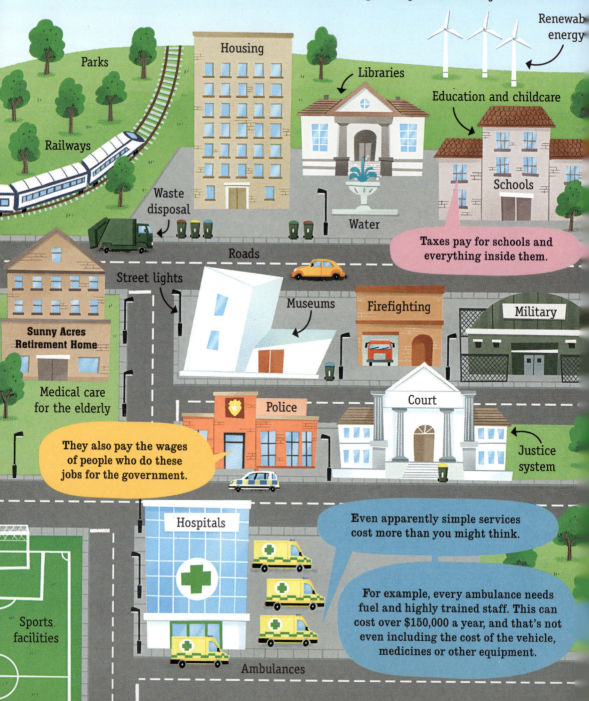

How to get more

If a government raises more money in taxes than it spends, it has a **surplus**. However, nearly all governments do the opposite – they spend more money than they raise, which leaves them with a **deficit**. When this happens most governments choose between two options, but both of them carry risks.

1) Borrowing

A government can borrow money from banks and other lenders. The total amount a government owes is called the **national debt**.

Most governments have a reliable source of income, from taxes, so banks like to lend them money. Borrowing money from banks can be an effective way for a government to raise funds quickly, so both sides are happy...

...but it's not sensible in the long term. Banks demand interest on the money they lend, and this can be very expensive. For example, in 2018, the US government spent around $390 BILLION of tax money, *just to pay back interest it owed.*

2) Printing money

If a government runs out of money, it can simply create more of its currency to pay for things. This might seem like an easy solution, but it's dangerous because a government maintains the value of its currency by *limiting* the money supply (see page 18).

This doesn't stop many governments from printing more money. Some do it because it's easier than raising taxes. Others do it for another, more complicated reason – find out more on page 101.

A *temporary* deficit isn't always a bad thing. Everyone relies on services the government provides – from roads and schools to hospitals and emergency services. If a government simply stopped spending when it ran out of money, it would be extremely damaging for both people and businesses.

Talking about taxes

People often disagree when it comes to taxes. Some think governments should raise taxes and spend more public money. Others want them to lower taxes and spend less. Here are some of their reasons.

Many people feel very strongly about how much money they want to pay the government in taxes. In countries where people can vote, it's often one of the main reasons why people support one particular political party rather than another.

Welfare

The support a government provides for its citizens is known as **welfare**. Almost every political party agrees it's good to spend *some* money on welfare, but it's harder to decide how much, or who deserves it.

> I worry a lot about getting so sick that I'd have to leave my job... How would I get money to live?

> Don't worry! Our government pays money to people who are too sick to work – or who can't find work for other reasons.

> Wait, what other reasons? I work hard. Why should I if the government is paying people to sit around?

> Who says anyone's sitting around? There are lots of reasons why people can't work. Maybe they have to care for their family, or they're too old to work.

> Maybe. But how do you know they're telling the truth? Why bother to work if you can lie and get money for nothing?

> You earn more money when you work! And the government doesn't give you an easy ride. They check on you to make sure you don't cheat the system – people who cheat go to prison.

> So the government also has to pay people to make sure no one's cheating? That's just more taxpayers' money going down the drain.

> Maybe... but what if the government paid EVERYONE a fixed amount to pay for their food and housing?*

*Some local governments in Canada and Finland have experimented with a program known as a **Basic Income**. Here, governments continued to *collect* taxes, but only from the rich. At the same time they also paid *everyone* a salary that would cover essential living costs, no matter how much they earned. Basic Income is an attempt to make welfare fairer – *everyone* gets the same amount, but only people who can afford it pay taxes. So far, experiments haven't shown if this can work across a whole country.

Keeping track

Most governments control their taxes and country-wide spending – but they *don't* control what people do with their money. The way people spend affects how much money a country makes and where it ends up – what's known as a country's **economy**. Each government keeps track of the economy so they can try to keep it stable.

One measure of a country's economy is called **Gross Domestic Product** or **GDP**. It's the total amount that all the goods and services in that country could be sold for – assuming people paid a fair price.

There are many sorts of goods and services. They all count towards GDP...

Food produced

Exports

Banks

Businesses

Making movies

Tourism

Making art

Stores

Online businesses

Restaurants

Natural resources

Factories

Education

GDP can be misleading. If lots of people live in a country, they'll produce lots of goods and services. This means a big country will often have a higher GDP than a small country, even if the small country makes more money for its size.

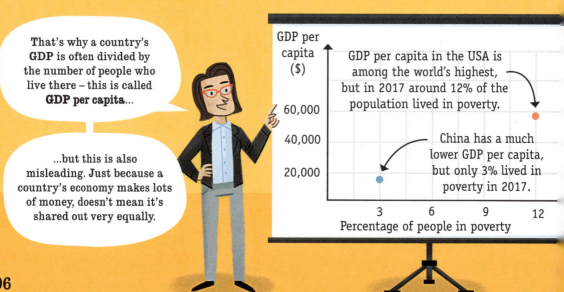

That's why a country's **GDP** is often divided by the number of people who live there – this is called **GDP per capita**...

...but this is also misleading. Just because a country's economy makes lots of money, doesn't mean it's shared out very equally.

GDP per capita in the USA is among the world's highest, but in 2017 around 12% of the population lived in poverty.

China has a much lower GDP per capita, but only 3% lived in poverty in 2017.

Price watch, wage watch

To get a better idea of how the economy is doing, governments track the prices of things people need to buy, and how much people earn.

It's impossible to monitor the price of *everything*, so governments focus on an imaginary shopping basket of things most people buy. Over time, these prices nearly always go up. When this happens, it's called **inflation**.

Governments also track how many people have jobs (the employed) and how many don't (the unemployed). They monitor people's wages, too: people will end up poorer if their wages don't go up as quickly as prices.

If wages and prices rise at the same rate...

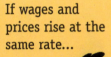

Monthly pay   Prices

...nobody really notices, and everyone can keep buying the things they need.

But, if wages *don't* go up as quickly as prices...

Monthly pay   Prices

...people end up worse off because they can't afford to buy as many things.

Managing the economy isn't an exact science, and economists argue about the best way to do it. But there are three ideas that most agree on:

> Spending is good! The more people spend, the more money businesses make, the more they can afford to increase their wages.

> Employment is good! People with jobs earn money to spend and pay taxes. And they're usually happier.

> Inflation is usually good, but not *too* much, and not *too* quickly.

97

The importance of inflation

Prices can rise and fall for many reasons. If they go up in just one store, it's not necessarily due to inflation and it probably won't affect many people. Inflation is when prices go up in most stores, in most places. It affects everyone, especially if it's out of control.

When inflation happens too quickly, wages can't keep up and money loses its value.

I budget $150 a week to spend on groceries for my family.

Now prices have rocketed, that money buys me much less.

People stop being able to afford many things. They're forced to make different decisions.

Last week $40 bought me a full tank, now it just buys me half. I might have to start taking the bus – it's cheaper.

Although a lot of inflation causes problems, governments still aim for a *little*. One reason for this is because the opposite can be *really* bad. If prices fall, it's known as **deflation**. That might sound appealing, but it has serious consequences.

Why bother buying it now? If you just wait a while it'll be cheaper and you'll save money.

Deflation encourages people to spend less. Businesses end up losing money, people lose their jobs – and this in turn means everyone ends up spending even less.

The government and the Fed

Governments need help managing the economy of their countries. Most work alongside a national institution called a **central bank** to help commercial banks and influence how much people spend. In the US, it's the job of the **Federal Reserve System** – or **the Fed** for short.

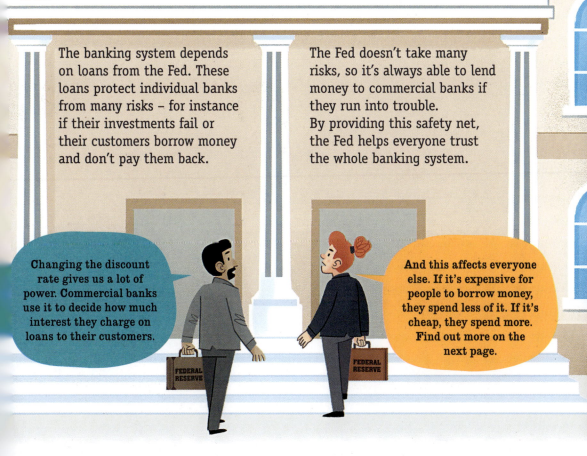

US law requires that all banks set aside a certain portion of their total money.

The money a bank sets aside is known as its **reserve**. If it doesn't have enough to meet the required reserve, the Fed can lend it the difference, with interest. The interest it charges is known as the **discount rate**.

The banking system depends on loans from the Fed. These loans protect individual banks from many risks – for instance if their investments fail or their customers borrow money and don't pay them back.

The Fed doesn't take many risks, so it's always able to lend money to commercial banks if they run into trouble. By providing this safety net, the Fed helps everyone trust the whole banking system.

Changing the discount rate gives us a lot of power. Commercial banks use it to decide how much interest they charge on loans to their customers.

And this affects everyone else. If it's expensive for people to borrow money, they spend less of it. If it's cheap, they spend more. Find out more on the next page.

A country's central bank is often **independent** of its government, but they both share their plans with each other and work together. One of their main projects is to manage inflation, so it stays at a steady rate. Turn the page to find out how they do this.

Managing inflation

Managing inflation is difficult because, in most countries, businesses are free to set their own prices. There are, however, a few ways in which governments and central banks can make a difference.

If inflation is too high...

The Federal Reserve can **raise** the discount rate, which is the interest it charges on loans to commercial banks.

Now it's more expensive for commercial banks to borrow from the Fed.

Commercial banks are more likely to raise their own interest rates, to cover these extra costs.

It becomes more expensive for people to borrow money from commercial banks.

If you took out a loan, you'd end up paying a lot of interest. Why not save up instead?

GREEN TREE BANK
We're here to help!

This encourages them to save instead of spend...

...which is bad for businesses.

Maybe I'll pass this time...

No one's buying anything. Maybe we should lower our prices?

So they respond by freezing their prices – or even lowering them.

Inflation **decreases**.

If inflation is too low...

The Fed can lower the discount rate.

Commercial banks lower their interest rates to attract customers.

People and businesses have more to spend.

Businesses put up their prices to increase profits.

Inflation increases.

Sometimes inflation is so low, changing the discount rate doesn't help.

MONEY TALKS — THE BIG DEBATE (Live)

"Rates of inflation are historically low. What can we do about this? Lower the discount rate?"

"We can't lower it any further – it's practically at zero..."

When this happens, the government and Federal Reserve can step in by creating new money, a process known as **quantitative easing**.

"Quantitative easing isn't simply printing money. There's more to it than that..."

First, the government borrows money from commercial banks.

Then the Fed creates new money to repay the commercial banks.

The discount rate is so low, commercial banks won't earn any interest if they hold onto this new money.

They invest it and loan it.

People have more money to spend.

Businesses increase their prices.

Inflation increases.

Taking control

There isn't just one way to manage a country's economy. Some people would like the government to have more control, so it can decide what happens to everyone's money. Others would like the government to leave the economy alone, and do nothing.

Total control

If a government had *total* control over the economy, we might not need money as we know it at all.

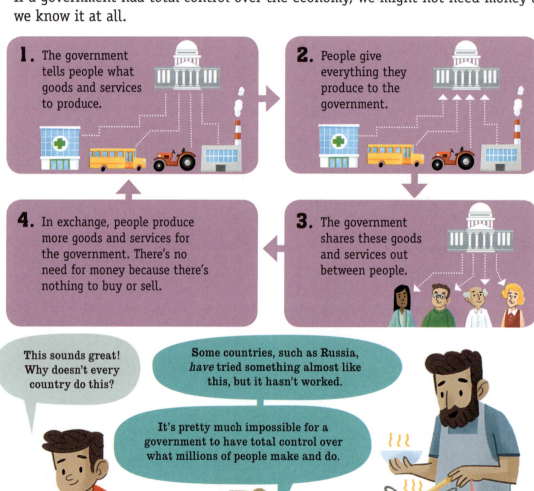

1. The government tells people what goods and services to produce.

2. People give everything they produce to the government.

3. The government shares these goods and services out between people.

4. In exchange, people produce more goods and services for the government. There's no need for money because there's nothing to buy or sell.

This sounds great! Why doesn't every country do this?

Some countries, such as Russia, *have* tried something almost like this, but it hasn't worked.

It's pretty much impossible for a government to have total control over what millions of people make and do.

But working together and sharing things out can still be very effective in small groups... Just like our family, in fact!

How much control?

In reality, no government has abolished money, or taken complete control over its country's businesses and trade. But equally, no government has left the economy completely alone. There are different degrees of control governments can take. What do you think is best?

More control

A government can try to force people and businesses to do what it wants.

- Use public money to buy businesses and take control over them.
- Force businesses to freeze their prices.
- Make laws that restrict what businesses can sell and what people can buy.

A government can leave people and businesses to make their own choices, but do things to *influence* these choices.

- Impose taxes and tariffs (see page 91).
- Offer tax breaks to people and businesses (see page 91).
- Use interest rates and quantitative easing to affect prices (see pages 100-101).

A government can step back completely, and do as little as possible.

- Take power away from the Federal Reserve and let prices rise or fall on their own.
- Lower taxes and abolish tax breaks to give people and businesses even more freedom.
- Stop providing welfare to people who can't afford to pay for things they need to live (see page 95).
- Give businesses more power than the government.

Less control

Chapter 7: Big questions

According to countless stories, songs and even religious beliefs, money can be both the source of great sadness, as well as a route to finding happiness. But is this because of money itself – or is it all to do with people's attitudes and beliefs about money?

No one knows the answer to this question, but in this chapter you can find out some of the ways people have tried to tackle problems relating to money, happiness and equality. To begin with, try to imagine a world in which people manage without money at all...

Do we still need cash?

More and more people no longer use cash to pay for things. They prefer to use a cell phone or bank card instead. At this rate, some countries, such as Sweden, are forecast to become cashless in the next 10 years. So do we need cash at all?

Paying with e-money...

✓ ...is often **quicker**, because neither side needs to count out coins or change.

✓ ...is **cheaper**: paper money costs a lot to produce and distribute.

✗ ...makes your money more **vulnerable** to attack from hackers.

✗ ...requires electricity, as well as an **expensive** device and the internet to work.

Cash...

✓ ...is **simple** and **accessible** – you don't need a bank account, phone or the internet.

✓ ...works in a **crisis**, such as a flood, because it doesn't need power or a network connection.

✗ ...makes people and businesses carrying it **vulnerable** to robbery.

...is **private**. You can spend cash without it leaving a digital record of what you're up to.
   On the flip side, it's hard for the police to trace criminals who use cash.

The key advantage of cash is that *everyone* can get their hands on it, even if they don't have an address, a bank account or a phone. Without it, about 1.7 billion people in the world wouldn't have access to money.

Do we need money at all?

Some people believe that money makes the world less fair – for example, some rich people can simply inherit money, while others, who work hard, can still struggle to get by. But there are alternatives to money that are much less easy to hoard.

Now imagine, for example, that you could pay for *everything* with time...

Nobody here is actually paying with their time. They're just trading units of time – in much the same way people pay with money. Maybe the problem we need to solve isn't money, but how we use it? Or maybe we've just not come up with the right alternative?

107

What about cryptocurrencies?

A cryptocurrency is a digital currency that is created, exchanged and kept safe using codebreaking – or **cryptography**. The first, known as **Bitcoin**, was created in 2009. Since then, many more have been made.

In February 2011, one virtual "coin" of Bitcoin (or ฿1) was worth $1. By December 2017, ฿1 was worth $19,783.

Here are two of the main reasons why they became so valuable.

Nobody is in charge

Most currencies are created and monitored by governments and banks. Cryptocurrencies are only created and exchanged by the people who use them (find out more on the next page) – no one else is involved.

Not everybody trusts banks or governments, especially since the 2008 financial crisis. Many people are excited by the idea of a currency that avoids them.

No secrets

There's a public record of every Bitcoin that has ever been created, and every Bitcoin transaction, known as a **blockchain**. Each entry on the blockchain is given a coded "fingerprint" that can't be changed.

This makes cryptocurrencies difficult to steal or counterfeit. If there's no record of a transaction on the blockchain, you know it's fake.

The system that protects Bitcoin is very secure. Hackers *have* found ways to steal Bitcoins, but it's very difficult, and often more expensive than it's worth.

Highs and lows

Twelve months after one Bitcoin was worth $19,783, its value had fallen to $3,183. The value of cryptocurrencies goes up and down regularly, and often drastically. As well as being unstable, there are other disadvantages, too.

They're hard to get and spend

There are two ways to get Bitcoins. You can buy them from somebody who has some, but that can be quite expensive. Or you can create your own by cracking a code...

Before a Bitcoin transaction is added to the blockchain, somebody has to crack a code. This is known as **mining** for Bitcoins.

The codes are so complicated, the code-crackers, or **miners**, have to use expensive, extra-powerful computer hardware.

The miner who cracks the code first is rewarded with new coins. A record of these coins appears on the blockchain.

Even if you manage to get some Bitcoins, they can't be spent everywhere. Not very many people or businesses accept Bitcoins as payment, and you can't exchange Bitcoins for another currency at a bank.

They're environmentally unfriendly

In November 2017 it was reported that Bitcoin-mining hardware worldwide used up more power than the entire Republic of Ireland did that same month.

That power was created by burning fossil fuels, which cause pollution.

Some people argue that cryptocurrencies aren't the problem – the power source is. If cleaner forms of energy were available, miners wouldn't produce as much waste.

109

Can money buy happiness?

Psychologists and economists have worked together to try to find out whether money and happiness are linked. One theory says it depends on the *kind* of happiness. You can imagine these as two different mountain peaks.

Day-to-day happiness

Measured by recording the emotions people feel each day

Life satisfaction

Measured by asking people to say how happy they are with their lives

> The more money people earn, the more likely people are to say they're satisfied.

> Once you earn enough to meet your basic needs, more money doesn't make you happier.

> Good health and friendships have a bigger impact than money on day-to-day happiness.

> Money and education both seem to make a bigger difference to life satisfaction than good health or friendships.

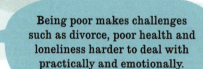

> Being poor makes challenges such as divorce, poor health and loneliness harder to deal with practically and emotionally.

> Well money doesn't *guarantee* happiness either way – some people have nothing and are perfectly happy, while others are rich and miserable.

> I don't know how I feel about this. Does it mean I need to try to earn lots of money?

> Let's just enjoy the view!

These are the results of a survey of 1,000 people in the US. What do *you* think?

110

Are rich countries happier?

Being richer tends to make people happier. But is it enough just to live in a country where most people are rich? This chart uses data collected by the World Bank to compare how rich a country is with how satisfied its population is.

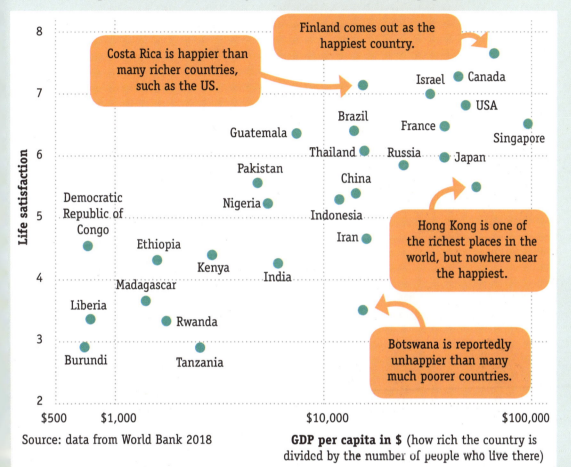

Source: data from World Bank 2018

This chart only provides a very simplified overview of what it's like to live in a country. But one thing it *does* suggest, is that even if richer countries *tend* to have more satisfied populations, this isn't always the case. So money isn't the only thing that makes people happy...

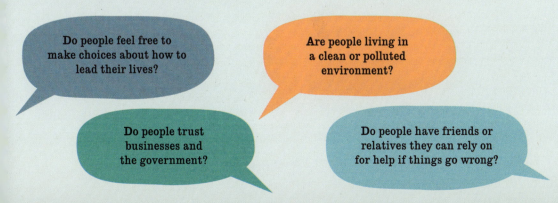

Is inequality bad?

Inequality is everywhere. Sometimes it doesn't matter – some people can wiggle their eyebrows, while others can't. But other times it seems really unfair, such as when some people have an excess of money while others live in poverty. When it comes to money, should we all be equal?

Imagine, for example, paying students in a school from a big pot of money. Here are three ways of sharing it out.

1. Everyone is paid the same, no matter what grades they get.

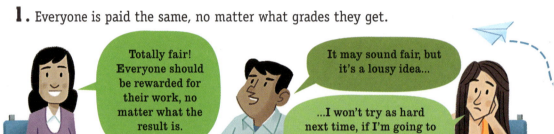

2. Only students with the top grades are paid, to encourage everyone to work hard.

3. Everyone gets something, but the better you do, the more money you get.

Which option would you choose? Would you choose any of them?

Lots of people tend to be ok with *some* amount of inequality – as long as it's not too extreme and everyone has a fair chance of reaching the top.

It's a silly example anyway, nobody actually gets paid for getting good grades.

Maybe not directly, but good grades *do* tend to lead to higher paying jobs in adult life...

In practice, it's hard to control how much inequality there is. In fact, the gap between rich and poor in most countries around the world is getting bigger – in some places faster than others. This happens for all sorts of reasons.

Money makes money
If you already have money, it's easier to make even more money from interest on savings and big investments.

Salary gap
People with power can, and do, give themselves big rewards, including the biggest salaries.

Discrimination
When people don't have the same opportunities, wages and rights because of their gender or race, it's known as **discrimination**. It's often illegal, but it's a fact of life for many people.

Tax havens
Wealthy people often find ways to pay less in taxes – making them richer and their governments poorer (see more on page 45).

There are as many different opinions about how to keep inequality in check as there are people.

Rich people create jobs and opportunities, so if we help *them*, we help everyone. The money trickles down.

It might help a little if the rich give money to the poor, but I think it's better to make sure we're all given equal opportunities from the start.

Poor people should take power from the rich!

If we forced everyone to share out their wealth more equally, we'd all be better off!

113

Dishonest money

One reason people like money so much is that it doesn't just allow you to buy *things*. It also has the power to open doors and influence *people*. So how do we make sure that it's not used for dishonest ends?

Money has the power to motivate people to change the world.

10 million dollar prize for the first person to design a battery that can power a car for as long as a tank of gas.

It can be used to influence the government, too.

A sugar company pays me to persuade politicians to make laws that will help their business. I'm a **lobbyist**.

Many people would agree it's OK to offer prize money to encourage innovation, and that it *can* be fair to hire lobbyists to influence governments. But both these ideas can be abused, and this is known as **corruption**. In most countries, governments set up anti-corruptions laws, but they don't always work.

Psst...Can you make sure my kid's university application goes into the right pile?

Paying to get around a rule or to get preferential treatment is known as **bribery**.

To help you win the vote, my country would like to give you some money.

But we're not allowed to accept donations from abroad!

Do you want to win or not? Imagine how many leaflets and ads you could pay for!

Ok, but let's keep it quiet! We're breaking the law.

Bad for everyone

Corruption is dishonest or illegal behavior by those who have money, and therefore power, to make things go in their favor. It causes inequality, and weakens people's trust in governments and businesses.

I don't bother voting in my country. The government will just do what big businesses want anyway.

Turning on the light

Corruption thrives behind closed doors, where people can act in secret. Governments can try to tackle it by...

...making laws that allow citizens and journalists to force organizations to share what they're up to, known as **freedom of information (FOI) laws**.

...making sure courts of law are free to try people – however rich or important they are.

...paying officials a fair wage, to make it less tempting for them to accept bribes.

...making sure people are open about when they're being paid to do something. For example, YouTubers need to say if they're being paid to promote a product.

...making lobbyists share information about what they do and how much they spend. This makes it easier to spot if corruption is taking place.

But if there are too *many* rules, people and businesses might struggle to follow them, and governments might struggle to keep track of everyone. So occasionally, *getting rid* of rules and paperwork can help too.

Protesting with money

When people decide not to buy something in protest, it's known as a **boycott.** That might seem like a small thing, but when lots of people act together it has a big impact. Here's a famous example.

At the beginning of the 20th century, India was under British rule. Britain made lots of money out of India – for instance, by taking control of its fabric industry.

Political campaigner Mohandas Gandhi encouraged Indians to boycott British products, in particular cloth, and make their own.

Nobody knows exactly how many people stopped buying British cloth, but as the boycott spread, more and more people began to support the independence movement. Many more years of protests eventually helped bring about Indian independence, in 1947.

This kind of protest – with money instead of violence – inspired many other people fighting for their rights all around the world.

The spinning wheel became a powerful symbol of Indian independence, even shaping the design of the Indian flag.

Consumer power

Consumer power is the idea that consumers can influence the decisions businesses make. Here are some more ways people do this.

Switch

Instead of not buying something, you can switch to a seller you prefer. Losing customers sends a signal to the seller.

Write

Writing a letter or social media post to a company lets them know about the issues their customers care about.

Donate

Give money to support organizations that campaign to make businesses behave better – for example by looking after the environment.

How to negotiate

One day, you might find yourself in a situation where you need to discuss a price in order to get a better deal. This is known as **negotiating**. Here are some tips for how to negotiate effectively – whether it's a record contract, a faulty item in a store or even a salary.

How to become a billionaire

One billion dollars is A LOT of money. To count to one billion, one number every second, would take over 30 years. How does anybody get their hands on that much money?

The billionaire baby
Wealth inherited from family

Starting money: Lots
Time taken: Rapid
Risk: Low
Success chances: High

The investor
Invested money until it grew into billions

Starting money: Medium
Time taken: Slow
Risk: Very high
Success chances: Low

The inventor
Invented something that kept on selling

Starting money: Varies
Time taken: Varies
Risk: Medium
Success chances: Very low

The entrepreneur
Businessperson who runs a big company or a few

Starting money: Varies
Time taken: Slow
Risk: High
Success rate: Low

Although anybody can become a billionaire, in practice most are over 55, grew up in a wealthy country, and graduated from a university.

Another important quality is persistence. Most billionaires fail, lose huge chunks of money, and have to try new things before they earn their riches.

There are no strict rules for how to earn a billion. You often hear about people who start with little and end up with lots – but that's because they make good stories. In reality, many billionaires have lots to begin with.

How much is enough?

Imagine you and four friends are each asked: "How much money would you need to live comfortably and happily for the rest of your life, with no other income?" Whoever writes the smallest amount gets the money. What number would *you* write?

You'd have to choose an amount *high enough* for you to buy basic necessities, but *low enough* to stand a chance of getting the money at all. How much somebody needs to live comfortably will vary from person to person.

I definitely want kids one day. That'll mean more mouths to feed.

The cost of basic necessities varies from place to place.

In my city, food and a place to live cost a lot!

A person who has to look after another person might need more than someone who doesn't.

To make your number lower, you would have to think hard about what you *really* need, and what you could do without.

My grandma says joy and fulfilment comes from within, and has nothing to do with how much money you have.

I might need care when I'm older, but I can definitely live without a trip to the movies every week.

I don't just want the necessities. Some extra spending would be nice. What do I like doing that doesn't cost much?

There's no right answer. It's also extremely unlikely you'll ever have to make this decision. But the question forces you to think of the lowest amount possible that would be "enough" for you. It'll probably be less than a billion!

What next?

By now you should have a sense that there isn't only one correct way to manage your money. Nor is there only one way to talk about it or even *think* about it. That's because money is an intensely personal subject. It's about how you relate to other people – your future plans, the work you do and, most of all, the promises you make.

At the same time, money is something that connects you to everybody else on the planet. As it changes hands from person to person or from business to business, another link is added to a chain of transactions that stretches back for thousands of years, reaching all over the world. This is why money matters.

Glossary

This glossary explains some of the words used in this book. Words written in *italic* type are explained in other entries.

asset any valuable item, such as a house or car or *bond* that can be sold to turn it into *liquid* money.

bank see *commercial bank* or *investment bank*

bank account a record of money deposited in a bank.

   checking account money you can access easily, at any time.

   savings account money you can only access sometimes, but that should earn greater *interest* than a checking account.

bankruptcy when a person is unable to pay their debts, and his or her possessions are sold off to pay back *creditors*.

bartering exchanging one thing directly for another, without using money.

billionaire someone whose total wealth adds up to at least 1 billion in their *currency*, for example $1,000,000,000.

bonds long-term *debts* sold by governments and big businesses.

boycott when many people agree not to spend money on a certain product, or a range of products made by certain businesses.

budget a written list of all income and expenditures, either for a person, a business or a government.

cash money in the form of coins or bills.

central bank see *Federal Reserve*.

collateral *assets* that *creditors* can collect from a person or business if they cannot repay a *debt*.

commercial bank a bank set up for individuals and businesses to save their money and apply for *loans*.

contract a written agreement, for example an employer agreeing to pay a particular *salary* in exchange for an employee doing a job.

costs money a business spends before it can sell its products.

counterfeiting making fake bills or coins.

credit money borrowed from a bank or business, that becomes *debt*.

credit card a card that allows a person to pay for things with *credit*.

credit rating a system used by banks to decide which customers they will give *loans* to, and at what price.

creditor a person, bank or business that *loans* money to another person.

cryptocurrency a digital *currency* that is created, exchanged and kept safe online, using mathematical and codebreaking techniques.

currency a system of money in general use in a particular place, such as British pounds or US dollars.

   currency exchange trading one kind of currency for another.

debit card a card that allows a person to pay for things by linking directly to a *bank account*.

debt money that is owed to a person, *bank* or business, typically to be repaid with *interest*.

   national debt money that is owed by a government to other governments or *banks*.

deficit when a business or government spends more money than it takes in.

deflation when prices in a country go down, on average.

derivatives any form of money whose value is derived from another form of money, such as a good, a service or an *asset*.

diversifying investing in several different things to minimize risk.

e-money an electronic form of *cash*.

economy the amount of money in a country, and how much that money is moving around within it.

Federal Reserve the US central bank, that controls the dollar and loans money to *commercial banks*.

finance to do with money, or the management of money.

financial instrument a *contract* between people, banks or businesses that relates to *cash*, *assets* or *derivatives*.

fraud lying to another person with the aim of getting them to give you money; usually a crime.

funding money needed for a business or project.

fundraising asking for money, usually to help pay for a charity or other good cause.

future a type of *derivative*, in which one person promises to pay an amount based on something that hasn't happened or doesn't exist yet.

GDP Gross Domestic Product, the total amount of *wealth* generated by all the people and businesses in a country.

gold standard an old system of money in which the value of a *currency* was linked to the value of a certain amount of gold.

inflation when prices in a country go up, on average, and when the value of a *currency* goes down.

insurance paying a small amount of money to a company that will help you pay back a large amount, in the event of an unpredictable event happening, such as an accident.

interest extra money you have to pay back to someone you have borrowed money from, and money that banks pay to customers with deposits.

   compound interest interest that adds to a *debt* if you don't pay off the exisiting *interest*.

interest rate the proportion of a *loan* that is charged as *interest*.

investing spending money on something, such as artwork or a *share* in a business, that you hope will increase in value.

investment bank a bank that governments, businesses or wealthy individuals use to raise money for expensive projects.

line of credit spending more money from a *bank account* than you have in that account.
liquidity the more easily money or *assets* can be collected and spent, the more liquid it is said to be.
loan money given to a person or business that has to be paid back, usually with *interest*.
loan shark a business or person that gives out *loans* illegally, often charging very high *interest*.

market a place where people can buy and sell things, or the people a business hopes to sell to.
mortgage a *loan* that allows a person to buy a house or other building and pay the *debt* back over many years.

quantitative easing when a government creates money, through *loans* from a *bank*, with the aim of increasing *inflation*.

philanthropist a person who gives away large amounts of their money to good causes.
poverty when people do not have enough money or income to afford basic needs such as food and shelter, and cannot get *loans*.
profit money gained by a business on top of what it costs to run that business.
public services things such as *welfare*, provided for everybody by a government, paid through *taxes*.

recession when the *economy* or *GDP* of a country gets weaker over a period of time.
regulations laws that make sure *banks* and businesses can't take big risks with other people's money, and to stop businesses from becoming too powerful.
retail bank see *commercial bank*

salary regular payment for doing a job, typically paid weekly or bi-monthly.
securities any form of *financial instrument* that one person can buy or sell to another, such as *shares*.
shareholder someone who owns *shares* in a business, and who can receive a portion of any *profits*.
shares parts of a business that are owned by different people.
stock market place where *stocks* and *shares* can be bought and sold.
stockbroker a person who is allowed to buy and sell in a *stock market*.
stocks another word for *shares*, although it technically describes a set of many shares.

taxes money that individuals and businesses pay to the government, to be spent on *public services*.

wage payment for doing a job.
wealth the amount of money a person or business has, including *assets* and *cash*.
welfare money paid by governments to provide basic services for people who cannot afford them.

Index

assets, 78
ATMs, 37, 38, 67, 77

bailouts, 50
bankers, 33, 50-51
bankruptcy, 65
banks, 5, 30, 35-51, 99, 100-101
   accounts, bank, 5, 36, 38, 76-77
   central banks, 18, 37, 99-101
   commercial banks, 35, 38-39, 48-49, 50-51, 99-101
   investment banks, 46-47, 48-49, 50-51
   run on the banks, 41
   vaults, bank, 30, 37, 38
bartering, 14, 24
basic income, 95
benefits, 55
billionaires, 119
bills, 19, 30-31
Bitcoin, 108-109
blockchain, 108-109
bonds, 32, 47, 78
borrowing, 7, 43, 58-65
boycotts, 116
brass, 28
bribery, 114
Britain, 31
bronze, 26-27, 28-29
budgets, 72
business loans, 59
businesses, 40, 46-49, 54, 90, 94, 98, 100-101, 103

carrots, 4, 14, 16
cash, 4, 16, 18-19, 37, 41, 106
cash machines, *see* ATMs
charities, 82-87

checking account, 76-77
China, 9, 27, 28, 30, 96
cocoa beans, 26, 27
coins, 19, 25, 27, 28-29, 30-31
collateral, 59, 65
compound interest, 61
consumer power, 117
corruption, 114-115
counterfeit money, 19, 30, 108
cowrie shells, 26, 27
credit cards, 5, 39, 58, 61, 64, 67
credit rating, 62-63
credit unions, 43
crime, 7, 29, 48, 51, 66-67, 68, 114
crowdfunding, 43, 83
cryptocurrencies, 108-109
currencies, 4, 8-9, 20-21, 93

debit cards, 5, 38, 67, 77
debts, 32, 48-49, 61, 64-65
deficit, 93
deflation, 98
deposits, 36-37, 38, 41, 76-77
derivatives, 33, 47
discount rate, 99-101
discrimination, 113
diversifying, 81
dividends, 78, 87
dollars, 8, 9, 20, 21, 29, 31
dolphin teeth, 26
donations, 6, 82-87

e-money, 4, 5, 16, 19, 37, 41, 106
earning, 6, 54-57, 79
economy, the, 96-97, 99, 102-103
embezzlement, 66
employee, 54, 55, 56, 57
employer, 55, 56, 57
employment, 54-57, 97
euros, 8, 20, 21

125

exchange rates, 9, 20
expenses, 72

Federal Reserve, the, 18, 37, 99-101
fiat money, 18, 31
financial advisors, 64-65
financial crisis, 48-51
financial instruments, 32-33, 47
First World War, the, 31
fraud, 66-69
freedom of information, 115
freelance work, 54, 55
fundraising, 82-83
futures, 33

gold, 28, 29, 30, 31
gold standard, the, 31
governments, 18, 21, 29, 31, 32, 44-45, 51, 89-103, 114-115
grain, 24, 25
Greece, ancient, 29
Gross Domestic Product (GDP), 96, 111

happiness, 110-111

income, 54, 56-57, 72, 79, 97
income tax, 90, 91
India, 28, 116
inequality, 112-113
inflation, 79, 97, 98, 100-101
ingots, 26
insurance, 75
interest, 32, 38, 39, 40, 42, 58, 60-61, 63, 76, 77, 79, 93
interest rates, 60-61, 76, 100-101
investing, 7, 46-47, 78-81
investors, 46-47
I.O.U., 25
Islamic banking, 42

jade, 26, 27
Jiaozi, 30
jobs, 49, 50, 54-56, 97, 98

laws, 115
lending, 7, 32, 39, 40, 42-43, 46, 48-49, 50, 58-63, 65, 93, 99, 100-101
line of credit, 58
liquidity, 17
loan sharks, 63
loans, 7, 39, 40, 48, 49, 59, 60, 63, 65
lobbying, 114, 115
Lydia, 28

medium of exchange, 15, 25
Mesopotamia, 24-25, 26
minimum wage, 57
money creation, 18, 21, 40-41, 93
money laundering, 66
money supply, 18, 93
mortgages, 39, 48, 49, 60
murabaha, 42
mutual funds, 81

national debt, 93
negotiating, 10, 55, 118

obsidian, 26
offshore banking, 44-45
online safety, 68-69
overspending, 74, 93

passwords, 67, 69
paying for things, 4, 5, 10, 14, 15, 30, 38, 106
paying without money, 14, 24-25, 107
peer-to-peer lending, 43
peppercorns, 26, 27
philanthropy, 86-87
phishing, 67, 68

piggy banks, 35, 38
politics, 21, 50-51, 94-95,
   102-103, 113, 114-115
pounds, 20, 21
poverty, 96
prices, 10, 74, 97, 98, 100-103
profit, 42, 48, 80
progressive taxes, 91
protests, 50-51, 116
public services, 6, 92, 95

quantitative easing, 101
quetzal feathers, 26

rai stones, 26, 27
receipts, 30, 72
recessions, 49
repayment, 39, 40, 42, 48, 49, 58,
   60, 62, 63, 64-65
reserve currency, 21
reserves, bank, 37, 99
retail banks, *see* banks, commercial
risk, 32, 62, 51, 78-81
Rome, ancient, 28
rubles, 9
Russia, 9, 90, 102

salary, 54
salt, 26
saving, 15, 61, 72, 76-77, 79, 100
savings accounts, 76-77
scams, 68-69
self-employment, 54
shares, 33, 46, 47, 78
shell companies, 44
silver, 25, 28, 29

spending, 6, 38, 72-74, 91, 94,
   96-97, 98, 100-101
stock exchanges, 47, 80
stockbrokers, 47, 80
stocks and shares, 33, 80-81
store of value, 15
supply and demand, 56
surplus, 93
switching, 117

talking about money, 11, 118
tariffs, 90, 91, 103
taxes, 6, 29, 44-45, 90-91, 92, 93,
   94, 95, 103
   tax breaks, 91
   tax havens, 44-45, 113
   tax rate, 91
tea, 26, 27
tipping, 10
transactions, 6-7
trust, 18, 19, 21, 25, 32, 108, 115

underwriting, 47
unions, 57
unit of account, 15, 25
UK, 31, 116
USA, 4, 8-9, 10, 20, 21, 31, 48-51,
   93, 96

wages, 91, 94, 97, 98
welfare, 95, 103
withdrawals, 37, 38, 41, 67
World Bank, 111
writing, 25, 27, 117

yuan, 9, 20, 21

Acknowledgements

Written by
Eddie Reynolds, Matthew Oldham
& Lara Bryan

Illustrated by
Marco Bonatti

Edited by
Alex Frith

Designed by Jamie Ball
& Freya Harrison

Money experts:
Museum on the Mound, *Edinburgh*
Martina Collett,
South Thames College, London
Young Money, *(part of young-enterprise.org.uk)*
Madalena Leão,
Treasury policy advisor

American editor: Carrie Armstrong
Series editor: Jane Chisholm

Series designer:
Stephen Moncrieff

The websites recommended at Usborne Quicklinks are regularly reviewed but Usborne Publishing is not responsible and does not accept liability for the availability or content of any website other than its own, or for any exposure to harmful, offensive or inaccurate material which may appear on the Web.

Usborne Publishing will have no liability for any damage or loss caused by viruses that may be downloaded as a result of browsing the sites it recommends.

First published in 2019 by Usborne Publishing Limited, 83-85 Saffron Hill, London EC1N 8RT, United Kingdom. usborne.com Copyright © 2019 Usborne Publishing Limited. The name Usborne and the Balloon logo are registered trade marks of Usborne Publishing Limited. All rights reserved. No part of this publication may be reproduced, stored in a retrieval system or transmitted in any form or by any means without prior permission of the publisher. First published in America 2019. This edition published 2023. AE.